No Better than I Should Be

BY THE SAME AUTHOR

Graham Came by Cleish
Late and Early
A Dictionary of the Bible
American Wit and Wisdom

with best wishes:
James L. Dow

James L. Dow

No Better than
I Should Be

THE MAKING OF A MINISTER

Foreword by Professor William Barclay

HUTCHINSON OF LONDON

Hutchinson & Co. (Publishers) Ltd
3 Fitzroy Square, London W1

London Melbourne Sydney Auckland
Wellington Johannesburg Cape Town
and agencies throughout the world

First published 1975
© James L. Dow 1975

Set in Monotype Times
Printed in Great Britain by The Anchor Press Ltd
and bound by Wm Brendon & Son Ltd
both of Tiptree, Essex

ISBN 0 09 121390 8

On ev'ry hand it will allow'd be,
He's just – nae better than he should be.
ROBERT BURNS:
A Dedication to Gavin Hamilton

Contents

Illustrations

Foreword

by Professor William Barclay, CBE, MA, DD

The name of Jimmy Dow is a household word in the West of Scotland. I have known Jimmy Dow for forty-five years. I have talked, studied, eaten, preached, played tennis and golf with him – and I think I know him pretty well.

The first and the most important thing about Jimmy is not that he is a minister of the church but that he is a human being. I once heard of a little girl who got the phrase 'human being' slightly mixed up. She insisted on talking not of 'human beings' but of 'human beams'. This would suit Jimmy very much indeed, for where he comes he brings the light of sincerity and of joy.

It is often the case that many who speak well do not write well. But this is not the case with Jimmy. He has written not only his autobiography but his own personality into his book. If I may tell the truth, when I was first asked to read the book I regarded the prospect of reading it as a chore which had to be done. I had not read a dozen pages before it was so fascinating to me that I found it difficult to lay down. One thing is true about Jimmy – all through life he has enjoyed himself and those who read this book will enjoy themselves too. I would make it compulsory reading for all students for the ministry, for all ministers and for all congregations. They need to hear what it is saying.

I have read this book with the greatest of pleasure and I wish it well and hope that very many will read it.

1. A Paisley Lad

Our oldest grandchild, Leslie, now owns the christening mug presented to me on my first birthday. I have no recollection of the ceremony. It is inscribed: 'To J. L. Dow, on his first birthday, from Grandpa and Grandma. 5:2:09.' This is a mistake.

I showed it to our daughter on one occasion, though normally it stood in the corner cupboard except on occasions when it was removed for cleaning, and asked her what the mistake was. She studied it long and hard and then said they had forgotten to put in my degree.

The mistake is that I was born not in February 1908 but in March, which makes me a Piscean and not an Aquarian, and this, no doubt, has had an important bearing on many events and tendencies.

I do not know what trouble Grandfather got into for getting the month wrong. I cannot remember Grandmother, but from a picture of the two of them which stood on the bookcase, I would think that the trouble was considerable. She is in black and all covered with sequins, with every hook and eye doing its duty, and wearing a little lace cap of a type favoured by Queen Victoria in her latter years. Grandfather is wearing, along with other garments, a Gladstone collar, and a pair of trousers that look as if they had been made in a plumber's. There is also the gold watch and chain without which no respectable working man would have ventured forth on the Sabbath day. The picture is completed by an aspidistra which looks as if it is growing out of the top of his head.

These were Father's parents; Mother and her brother had been left orphans when they were very young. And since Father was an only child, we were not, in the later life, troubled by many relatives. This was a bit of a handicap at Christmas, but there are compensations, and one must learn to take the smooth with the rough.

Grandfather and Grandmother lived in a cottage at the foot of Taylor's Wynd in Dundee, and I never smell bleach without thinking about it. Bleach, jute, and Dundee are forever associated in my mind.

Grandfather was a stonemason to trade, and when we went to see him he would take me out for a walk, clinging to his horny hand in case I got knocked down by a horse, and he would point out buildings whose foundation stone he had laid with the assistance of provosts and other dignitaries. His hands were so hard that he could lift a coal out of the fire with his fingers to light his pipe, producing an aroma of thick black and another which would have told a cannibal that his dinner was overdue.

Father served his time as a land surveyor and came to Paisley around the beginning of the century to the county service. Mother followed later and they were married, taking a house in Mavisbank Terrace, which was the last row of tenement houses on the low road to Barrhead. We were really in the country. And there I was born.

I do not suppose that there is any connection between that event and the founding of the Boy Scout movement, but they did occur at the same time. Father immediately fell for it. Maybe he thought his second son was going to need something of the sort. He had been a founder-member of the 1st Dundee Company of the Boys' Brigade, which is, of course, an organization older than the Scouts. When he came to Paisley he continued his interest. But he must have got carried away with this new thing. He formed the first Boy Scout troop in Paisley. Living in Arran there is a man who was my father's first patrol leader. He has told me that he remembers me at Mavisbank, a bouncing baby lying on the hearthrug.

There are mothers and fathers who actually used to have their offspring photographed, stark naked, lying face down on hearthrugs. Mine, I am thankful to say, never did.

My brother is three and a half years older than I am, which means that neither of us was old enough to join the Scouts in 1908, but we were brought up in the highest traditions of the movement, one of our earliest toys, no doubt, being two pieces of wood to rub together to light fires. I probably chewed mine. They have told me that as a child I chewed everything from the *Children's Encyclopaedia* which was then appearing in weekly instalments, to a bread poultice which had been applied for some juvenile disorder.

Mavisbank Terrace still stands, solid, substantial, the best type of tenement building (though now referred to as 'flets') but a type which were not approved by socialist town councils, some of whose members had recollections of the worst type of Scottish tenement, than which there was nothing worse.

Although I have tried very hard, I cannot recall anything about my first four years in this vale of tears. I do remember being taken to see Colonel Cody (not Buffalo Bill, but another of the same name) who was to fly a plane from Scotstoun showground. Off we went in the blue car, crossed Renfrew Ferry and walked to Scotstoun. Unfortunately the rain came on and the flight was cancelled. We went back on the next Saturday and saw him circle the field to the plaudits of the crowd. Many of them, I suppose, thought that there was no future in this means of transport.

I also remember seeing the *Aquitania* on the stocks at John Brown's Clydebank yard. That must have been 1913.

About this time we removed from Mavisbank to Greenlaw Avenue at the other end of the town. My brother Lex was ready for school by this time, and the avenue was handier to the Paisley Grammar which was to be entrusted with the responsibility of educating us. In Greenlaw Avenue I made my first real friend, Johnnie Lawrie. Johnnie and I went to school together in 1912, though I think he went a day or two earlier. We were on holiday for the whole month of August, and hadn't got back in time. I would be four and a half.

Miss Miller, the infant mistress, welcomed me. Possibly the Rector was not available at the time. She asked me if there was anyone I would like to sit beside. I pointed to Johnnie. Ten minutes later we were separated, never again to sit together in that class.

In those days concentration was on the three R's, and I am not going to engage in any controversy over the methods of yesterday and today, or to make odious comparisons. But we did learn to spell, and to read, and to count. At least some learned how to count: it is an art which somehow has eluded me.

Ours was the last close in Greenlaw Avenue and over the garden wall was a sizable piece of vacant ground which we called the Park, and where we played our games. One favourite was to stand in a circle heaving a brick from one to the other. This was to make us big and strong. On one occasion Johnnie heaved it to Bertie adding, possibly inadvertently but certainly unwisely, the words, 'Hit it with your head, Bertie.'

Bertie must have been a biddable boy, or half-witted, or something for he rose to it like a bird. Thereafter he was conveyed to the house of a neighbour who swathed him in bed-sheets till the doctor arrived on his bicycle and did him up in fairy stitch. We waited for the last rites, and tried to console Johnnie with the information that hanging was practically painless. Being his friend I told him that the worst that could happen to him was to be sent to a training ship.

I knew about training ships, for there was an old ship of the line by the name of *Mars* which was moored on the Tay, and I had on occasion been told by Mother that this was where I would end up if I didn't behave myself. Possibly East Coast readers will recall the ballad:

> There is a training ship
> On the river Tay.
> Where they get ham and eggs
> Three times a day.
> Oh, how the *Mars* boys yell
> When they hear the dinner bell.
> They run down the stairs like hell
> On the river Tay.

That is the way Uncle Fred sang it, and I preferred it to Father's version which had the boys running down the stairs pell-mell. But Uncle Fred was not a Boy Scout. Either version was better than the one which referred to a happy land, far, far away, and which was sung to the same tune. An obvious parody.

Of course we played the usual street games. Men of my age who ought to know better at their time of life are constantly bewailing the disappearance of street games. The modern child can't play in the street without ending up in hospital. Our only threat to life and limb was a horse-drawn-coal lorry. When you saw a motor car you ran for the pavement, and stood there fascinated.

The disappearance of the horse-drawn lorry is to be regretted for many reasons, one of which is that it has denied to the modern boy a source of much innocent pleasure. You got a box – a boot box being the most suitable – and filled this with what the horse had left behind when it had finished its dinner. You then wrapped up the box carefully in brown paper just as the man in the shoe-shop does, and left it on the wall, neatly tied with string. You then disappeared to an upstairs window and waited.

There were those who, like the Priest and the Levite, passed by on the other side, being either models of rectitude, or having a solid Presbyterian fear of the police. But sooner or later one would come, look at the parcel, look all round, then pick it up and walk smartly off with the appearance of one who had left it there for safe keeping until he came back.

Of course we never saw the end of this, but we speculated on it, and this stimulated the imagination. We always hoped that the man would open it when his family were just sitting down to their tea.

There were other games: hunch-cuddy-hunch, turn-the-pie, relievers, rounders, and, of course, football unlimited. 'Clockwork' was a favourite. You climbed up to a window, inserted a pin in the sash and attached thereto a thread with a coat button tied to it. You climbed down, paying out the thread, and concealed yourself. You then manipulated the thread so that the button tapped on the window.

Fathers who had done it themselves in their day merely opened the window and broke the thread. It was better to select a house occupied by the elderly, or by a widow. The elderly would look out of the window fearfully; the widows hopefully.

In Primary One I got a prize. There was nothing remarkable in this. Everyone in Primary One got a prize. This was intended, no doubt to give us a taste for this kind of thing, and to spur us on to higher endeavour.

In Class Two also I got a prize, this time strictly on merit. The family were delighted. They saw the book; in fact Mother saw the presentation, which was as well, for it was the last for a considerable time. The book was Percy F. Westerman's *The Flying Submarine*. A day or two later a chap asked me for a read of it, and I have never seen it since. I think he must have emigrated.

It was in Class Three, however, that I first tasted the heady wine of literary success. As always in such tastings, there was a hangover. Miss Love was the teacher. She required us to write a story, and I wrote a very good story. I thought so, and Miss Love agreed. It was about something exciting, like a fire, or an explosion, or a train crash. I can't remember. I only know that it was very good. Miss Love said so. I had put my heart and soul into it. The thing was quite dramatic.

Miss Love must have thought that after all these years this was the breakthrough. This was what made all the sufferings and frustrations of a school teacher worthwhile. Here was a boy, under eight years of age, in whose breast the flame of genius burned. At least the spark was there. She would fan it into flame, and then, when I had become poet laureate or prime minister, or something, she would be able to say: 'I was there at the beginning'.

She read the story out to the class as an example of what she had been looking for. Her eyes were shining. I tried to look modest and to convey the impression that I did this kind of thing every day; or at least three times a week. The wee girl who lived in the house above us was gazing at me with a look of adoration. At least I thought it was adoration. It may have been calculation.

Then a little twerp, whose name I have erased from the tablets of my memory in case something terrible has happened to him and I would feel responsible if I remembered who he was, held up his hand. I thought that it was no more than that the story had excited him so much that he was moved to seek permission to leave the room. Instead of that, and in reply to Miss Love's inquiry, he said that the story had been in last year's *Chatterbox*.

Of course it had been in last year's *Chatterbox*, but I had not copied it. Last year's *Chatterbox* was at home. I had written, and, I thought, improved it, from memory. How was I to know that he got *Chatterbox* too? And, anyway, why hadn't he remembered the story and rewritten it for Miss Love? Then I would have been able to hold up my hand and to say: 'Please, miss, that story was in last year's *Chatterbox*.' It was all very humiliating.

2. Kaiser Bill and Others

Elsie was born in 1913: she has now given up trying to conceal her age, so she won't mind my giving it away. And next year war broke out; though there was no connection between the two events. Father was desperate to get away. Of course all the best types in the country were desperate to join up. They were volunteering by the thousand, to be condemned by some of the worst brains in the country to their death. A generation was wiped out which was never to be replaced, and what the cost of that was to the country and to the world, nobody will ever know.

They turned Father down for what was called in those days a smoker's heart. This nearly broke his, and it did put an idea into his head that he was a sick man who hadn't long to live. Neither he had, but I think it was the idea that was more than a little responsible for that. He did the next best thing, and joined the Volunteers, the 'Dad's Army' of the First World War. And never let it be forgotten that although folk laughed at the Volunteers sometimes, as later they laughed at the Home Guard, these men would have laid down their lives and given a very good account of themselves had the call come.

They gave him a uniform that certainly was not made to measure, and puttees that wouldn't stay up, and boots that I dubbinned for him, and a rifle which we were allowed to clean under strict super-vision in case we broke it. He would come home after parade, having learned some new and more terrible way of killing Germans, and would demonstrate this to his fascinated offspring. While he was performing 'guard, butt, point, smash', Mother would be sitting with her knitting, doing 'in, over, through, off'. It fairly brought the war home to us.

I remember very clearly a big parade of Volunteers. They were to be inspected at Paisley Cross by a field marshal or something, and were then to march down the Glasgow road and dismiss in Green-law Avenue, which was a fine broad road, suitable for manoeuvres of this sort. There was a great polishing of buttons and pulling through of rifles, and away Father went to the parade ground. We awaited their return, allowing a suitable interval for the field marshal to make appropriate remarks.

Then in the distance we heard the strains of the band, and swinging into our view came the Volunteers, rank after rank of grim deter-mination, except for a few who looked as if they had other things on their mind, like their puttees becoming unravelled. Unfortunately this must have been a band from Glasgow who didn't know where Greenlaw Avenue was. They marched straight on in the general direction of Maryhill barracks, while the battalion did a smart left wheel into the avenue – they being Paisley to a man – and with all the expertise of men who had done it once before or who remembered something from their Boys' Brigade days. They drew up in rigid line while the strains of the band faded in an easterly direction.

The recognized way for a band to stop playing is for the drum major to give a sign to the big drummer, who thereupon gives the drum a double dunt. Then they all stop at the end of one bar and head for the nearest one. This was not how this band stopped. They did it *seriatim*. It was like that orchestral piece of Haydn's where the instrumentalists blow out their candles one by one, and depart like the Arabs after they have folded their tents. The last man in was the big drummer who had not quite picked up what the adjutant, who had gone haring after the band, had said. He was a dedicated man, or stone deaf, or something, but he stopped eventually. Possibly they shot him. A very subdued band walked back to Greenlaw Avenue and tried to hide up a close.

Our minister went to the war: he was Joseph Johnston, and about all I remember of him is that he never wore a clerical collar. When he came back after having done his stint with Huts and Canteens, or YMCA, or something similar, Father felt that something of an occasion should be made of this. Everybody who had been to France must, in his view, be a hero. The occasion was to be the annual Sunday School *soirée*. Some pronounced it 'swarrie', others 'suree'. No Frenchman would have known what was meant anyway.

Father wrote some verses, and Miss Aitkman's class were instructed to learn one verse each. On each juvenile's back there was tied a placard, bearing a letter of the alphabet. One by one they made their entrances, making sure the audience did not see the letter on the placard, and most of them making sure the audience didn't hear the words. Each one, having said his piece, lined up with the others, and stood still, except for the inevitable one who was needing the bathroom.

The dénouement was to be that when the last had made his contribution, the whole line would do a smart about-turn, and the audience would read on their backs the letters making up the words WELCOME HOME.

For once, I was not taking part in this extravaganza, but was up at the back with Father to get the full effect. It was more an impact. I can remember the look on his face yet.

The last verse of this deathless piece of poetry was:

> You fought the fight, you did your bit
> From Ypres to the Somme.
> Accept our thanks and hear us
> As we wish you Welcome Home.

Whereupon they turned round smartly and presented the cabalistic message EMOH EMOCLEW. Miss Aitkman had put them on at the wrong side of the stage.

I have mentioned Sunday School without having mentioned church and our church connection, though, of course, this is important. When Father came from Dundee he took digs near the County Buildings in the north of Paisley, and joined St James' Church. St James' was of the United Free persuasion and was attended by a rather well-to-do congregation. That was not what attracted Father. It was the minister, Dr Walton, a very distinguished man. He baptized me, which is not part of the distinction, but I cannot remember him.

Oddly enough, however, St James' was built in a far from salubrious part of the town, and its contact with the people who lived there was more a missionary one than a congregational one. There were two Sunday Schools. One met in the afternoon, and was mainly for the children of members. The other met at ten in the morning and was for the children round the doors. Father became a teacher in this school, and by the time we were ready for religious education he had become superintendent.

It was a fair walk from Greenlaw Avenue to St James' Church, but not as far as from Mavisbank Terrace to church. We moved back to Mavisbank to a top storey which had two large attics. One of these was allocated to me and the other to brother Alexander, known as Lex. We attended the morning Sunday School. It is a good hour for a Sunday School to meet, though I have never been able to persuade Sunday School teachers that it is so.

3. Sailor Suits and Sunday Schools

Boys nowadays seem to pass straight from nappies to long trousers: not so in my day. There was a long time to spend in short trousers before you graduated to the longs, and unless you were very tall, which I was not, this would not be under the age of fifteen or thereabouts. Of course, if you wore a sailor suit, and were an officer, it was different.

At one stage I wore a sailor suit, but I was not an officer. I was not even a petty officer. I was an ordinary seaman, wearing a round cap with HMS *Nelson* on the band. There was a dark blue blouse and a light blue collar with three white stripes on it. In addition there was a white lanyard with a wooden whistle, for calling the watch, splicing the mainbrace, or signalling for a penalty kick. But if you were an officer it was different. Then you wore long trousers, and a cap with a skip, and a reefer jacket with brass buttons and gold braid. It was very humiliating when on a Sunday you met a little twerp from the next street, dressed like this, and had to salute him.

But when I say that for me it was short trousers all the way, I mean 'all the way'. For Mother was an economical soul and bought things for our growth. By the time they fitted us they were done. Maybe I was a slow grower.

Underneath the short trousers, which were anything but short, there was an interesting garment called combinations. I see them depicted occasionally in the small advertisements in popular daily newspapers. They seem to have been issued to the American Army at some time. They were worn next the skin, and, since they, too, had been bought for your growth, they always hung down. When they were done they ended their useful life washing the stairs. No doubt they were warm and suitable garments, but no one could

say, even by the wildest stretch of the imagination, that they were
glamorous. They had a wee flap at the back.

There was an occasion when the medical officer was to call at the
school and I forgot to tell Mother. It was a Monday, when the good
combinations were in the wash, and the less reputable pair was on
me. When the report came in with an account of my general state of
health there was a footnote which read 'Underclothing inadequate'.
It was then I discovered that there was another use for the wee flap
at the back. James had dragged the Dow name, once more, in the
mire.

Nevertheless I will say that when the modern boy appears in
shorts for some purpose or another he displays knees as white as
wally door-knobs. Long trousers, like charity, cover a multitude of
shins. In the Book of Samuel there is some account of a woman by
the name of Abigail, who is described as being of 'good understanding'. I do not suppose that the writer was referring to her legs,
but in that sense I was a boy of good understanding. Had I entered a
beauty competition (a thought which never entered the mind of
my parents or of myself) it would have been my knees that the
judges would have concentrated on. Not because they are beautiful:
just because they are different. They would stand out a mile in a
beauty competition. In a riding school they would be accepted as
normal. But the subject was dress, and the Sabbath day.

After I graduated from the sailor suit, without winning promotion,
they dressed me in a kilt, and I loathed it. The modern boy may
wonder why a Scotsman should loathe the kilt. But he wears the
emancipated kilt which came in between the Wars when the hiking
cult developed: a kilt that can be worn with an open-necked shirt, or
a jersey, or, at worst, a tweed jacket. This was not my kind of kilt.

It had a kind of bodice sewn on to the top of it, like a waistcoat.
This was to keep the kilt from falling down. Over this you wore a
blouse, and then a green waistcoat, and, on top, a green cutaway
jacket, both with lozenge-shaped white metal buttons, which always
caught in your sister's hair any time she came near you.

Round the neck you wore a washable Eton collar and a tartan
bow tie. The stockings were tartan too, and the shoes had buckles
which you pretended were solid silver. On the head you wore a
Balmoral, known colloquially as a bumroller, and from behind a

cairngorm brooch there uprose what had once been a blackcock's stern. The sporran was the front part of an unidentified animal which might have been a beaver. I loathed the whole outfit.

As a matter of fact it was the cause of my running away from home for the first and only time in my life.

We were going to Broughty Ferry on holiday just about the end of the First War, and for travelling I was arrayed in this outfit which I have painfully described. It is known as the garb of old Gaul. The Gauls were, originally, the Galatians, and I am sure that if they had dressed themselves the way I was dressed they would have got a stronger letter from the Apostle Paul.

When we got to Broughty Ferry I asked politely (I would have got a clip on the earhole if I had not asked politely) if I might rid myself of these habiliments, and array myself in something more suitable for the mood of holiday. I was told that this would not be possible until the hamper was unpacked, and to go out and play.

Imagine any Christian, however tender in years, going out to play, on the first day of his holidays, and among complete strangers, looking like a cross between Harry Lauder and Little Lord Fauntleroy. I decided to run away from home, and in the morning they would find my cold dead body, and then they would be sorry. For all I cared, they could bury me in the kilt. I set out in a northerly direction.

Eventually I reached Buddon, where there was a military establishment. After they had fed me and watered me they had a committee meeting. I was not old enough for a court martial. A lance-corporal suggested that I might be adopted as the regimental mascot, but a sergeant pointed out that they already had a goat. They returned me to what I hoped were my conscious-stricken parents. It was not their conscience that got stricken, however. The kilt, like combinations, has disadvantages, though in reverse. The flap of the combinations comes down, the kilt lifts up.

But we must get back to church, which would be a splendid thing for a great many people to do.

In my early days there was not, of course, the practice where all the young children sit together at the front, and troop out immediately after the children's hymn which follows the children's address. You came in at the beginning and you sat it out till the end, and we had done an hour in Sunday School before that.

The practice of the 'Primary' going out half-way through was introduced for the best of reasons, as most doubtful practices are introduced. It would allow parents of young children to get out to church together; the 'Beginners' Department', being more or less a crèche. But it did kill the family pew, and it weakened the start of the habit of churchgoing.

It is an interesting reflection that in all my forty-odd years in the ministry (and some of them have been very odd) I have never had any difficulty in recruiting Primary Sunday School teachers. Not since the day when the Primary pupils started going out before the sermon and the offering.

It was hard, however, to get teachers for the Junior and Senior Schools which met after service at half past twelve. I know one minister who, faced with this difficulty, decided that all children of all ages should go out after the children's address. He finished up with more teachers than he had pupils.

I have mentioned one Sunday School *soirée*. There was one every year. It took place in the winter or the spring. The summer event was the Sunday School trip. At the *soirée* the prizes were handed out for attendance coupled with proficiency in Christianity, and you had to be reasonably well behaved or you got chucked out before the tea came on. We were always well behaved, since Father was superintendent. We usually got prizes for proficiency, and always for attendance. Of course, we had no option.

Each class was supposed to do a turn at the *soirée*. Some wee lassie would sing a song she got at day school, and since half of the audience went to the same school, it lacked novelty. Or it might be a recitation, or a carefully rehearsed sketch; always with a moral attached. It didn't really matter, for in the audience nobody could hear the words from the stage. They were drowned by the mothers supplying the prompts from the body of the hall.

This entertainment was followed by the tea and comestibles, which were contained in a paper bag, made up by the baker. You received this on surrender of your admssion ticket, thus making it impossible to obtain two bags, unless you had two admission tickets, which was unthinkable, since they cost fourpence. The bag contained four items, never less, and never more.

There was one paris bun or one coffee bun. The former had never seen Paris and the latter hadn't seen much coffee. There was one fruit cake or tart (never both) and one indeterminate, but mainly gingery, bun usually with icing on top. And there was a segment of a confection known as a Loch Katrine cake. It was iced on one side, and looked like a triangular tombstone. On the bottom was something that looked and tasted like wet wrapping paper, and which may have been wet wrapping paper for all I know. You washed this down with a special brew of tea unknown at any function other than a Sunday School *soirée*. It had been stewed by the church officer for most of the afternoon with the milk and sugar added.

Father would open the proceedings with a pessimistic appeal to the hungry gluttons to refrain from getting their mouths full until the minister, who was there only because it was expected of him, had asked the blessing. Father would then ask us to keep all the empty bags to the end, when, after a count of one, two, three, we would burst them all in one splendid and concerted bang.

I used to wonder why Father wasted his time on this useless appeal when he knew full well that nobody had the very slightest intention of paying any attention to it. The whole pleasure in blowing up paper bags and bursting them is in the timing of the burst. Just when the minister is reaching the punch line in some anecdote about John Knox or the Apostle Paul, or some other exemplary character whom we ought to model ourselves on, is the time to burst a paper bag.

After the *soirée* was over, and by a tradition as immutable as the laws of the Medes and the Persians, you got an orange as you went out of the door. These came, I am sure, from a special orange grove near Seville where they were grown for Sunday School 'swarries' or for the manufacture of marmalade.

4. The Summer Trip

In the summer came the Sunday School trip, an event to which three men looked forward with little joy: the superintendent, the minister, and the church officer. They remember what happened last year and the year before that, and they know it will undoubtedly happen again. The day may be fine (which is unusual), it may not be fine (which is normal), but the same things will happen again.

For the trip during the First War we walked from the church to Ferguslie Park, the seat of one of the Coats family of thread-mill fame. We wore our tinnies round our neck, and marched behind the Boys' Brigade band. There were lorries with forms tied on them to accommodate the infirm, those with young children, and any boy who managed to climb up while the authorities were not looking. We never dreamed of doing this. Father was superintendent.

After the War we went to more foreign parts like Inverkip and Kilmun, and even Ettrick Bay. There always had to be an advance party, nominally under the command of the church officer. It was made up of younger teachers who had been down at the church hall on the Friday night looking for the gear which had not been looked at since the last trip. This usually involved a great deal of searching in the belfry; the most efficient search party consisting of one teacher of each sex.

They were placed in charge of the various hampers of gear and provisions on the Saturday morning and sent on ahead to get things ready. The church officer had seen to it that a sackful of bobbin sticks by courtesy of the thread mills, had been delivered to the church hall. Of course when the advance party arrived, say at Blairmore, it was discovered that the bobbins were still in Paisley. But, kindling or no kindling, the water in the boiler still has to be boiled.

By the time the main body arrives, clamouring for tea and sausage rolls, the water is still not boiling, though the church officer is fast approaching that point. For the last three hours he has been doing his best with flotsam and jetsam from the shore, whin bushes, and a pail of coal borrowed from the piermaster who had got it as a present from the chief engineer of the *Marchioness of Breadalbane.*

But every time the steam beings to trickle out and he is standing by with the tea-bags (if he has remembered to bring the tea-bags) the cold wind blows on the boiler and it goes off the boil again. So the superintendent consults the minister, who is wishing that he was home getting ready for tomorrow, and they decide to have the races now and the tea later.

This is the sign for all the elderly ladies and the young ones with folding prams to spread rugs and blankets on the only flat bit of ground in sight and to open vast bags of provisions supplied by themselves as extra to the official rations, to sustain their brood who have been stuffing themselves with macaroon bars and lemonade since leaving Paisley St James' Station. In spite of loud protests and claims that they were there first, they are persuaded to move to the sidelines so that battle may commence.

The great game at a Sunday School trip is rounders. Why this should be so, I know not. I merely state it as a fact. The only other people who play rounders are Americans and they call it baseball. There must have been a Sunday School trip to New England in the days of the Pilgrim Fathers.

The young male teachers try to show off in front of the young female teachers, and are determined to belt the ball out of the park. Inevitably they miss it and try to make fleetness of foot compensate for deficiency of vision. They dash for the first base, and slip. This is always at a place where a cow had been ruminating earlier.

There is always trouble with the races. Just about as much trouble as the United Nations have. I am convinced – and other ministers, to a man, have confirmed this – that parents of children attending a Sunday School trip believe that on the Friday night the teachers hold a meeting behind closed doors and decide who are to win the prizes.

Picture the scene, then, unless perchance you too have suffered. There is a double row of spectators, grannies, mothers, sisters, brothers, and even the occasional father. I do not mean that he is a father only occasionally, but that he does not attend Sunday School trips with any regularity.

The minister is the starter, and he is willing at risk of life, limb, and the bonus he is always hoping for and never gets, to see to it that justice is not only done, but is seen to be done. He announces the first race: 'Girls, Primary, four years and under,' and at once is nearly submerged beneath a shrieking mass of maidenhood. These are the enthusiastic ones, accompanied by their big sisters who are protesting that they know for a fact that Susan McMenamie was five the day before yesterday.

Others of the permitted age are standing sucking their thumbs, waiting to be coaxed. But eventually they are dragged to the starting post by the hair of the head. The minister hopefully explains the rules, to which no one pays the slightest attention, blows his whistle and the two-thirty is off. He breathes a brief intercessory prayer for the superintendent who has to select the first three at the other end, and calls for Boys, Primary, four.

And so it goes on as the day wanes and the shadows lengthen, race after race through the seven ages of man and woman. The married women's race, which they run in their stocking soles, since their stilettos cost them the title last year at Kilmun; and the grannies' race, which has to be carefully handicapped since there are grannies of forty and grannies of eighty. Mrs McBride wins again, having started an odds-on favourite, being asked to cover only three yards.

The church officer announces that the tea is ready. The minister hands the whistle back to the superintendent, and borrows a mouthful of ginger beer from a youth who looks as if he is about due to get rid of what he has drunk already. He seeks out his fellow sufferer, the church officer. Two minds with but a single thought: is it nearly boat time and will they manage to get down to see the engines without the session clerk seeing them?

5. Classroom Cowboy

I have already mentioned an early excursion into literature and my humiliation when it was revealed that a story in *Chatterbox* had been my inspiration. Oddly enough I did something similar in Class Four, but, possibly in atonement, I attributed authorship to another person.

On my ninth birthday I was given a present of a revolver of the pattern favoured by Big Bill Hart, the cowboy hero of the day. Along with it came two instructions: how to put the caps in, and not to take it to school. But what pleasure is there in having a revolver of the type favoured by Big Bill Hart when it cannot be seen by boys who do not have one? I took it to school.

While Miss Gray's back was turned I produced the weapon and did some fancy shooting round the class. It was then that I made an interesting discovery. If a teacher wearing glasses is looking at the blackboard her glasses act as mirrors. I was bidden to the judgement seat, and the revolver was confiscated and placed in her desk adjacent to the coiled-up strap. This, of course, greatly delighted all the other boys, who were then persuaded that there is a certain rough justice in life after all.

At lunchtime I asked Miss Gray for the return of the revolver, which she refused. Now here was a thing! Not to be seen playing with the revolver at lunchtime I could get away with; we didn't have much time at home. But four o'clock was different. Questions would be asked, awkward questions, for which I could think of no answer, even though I had a fairly fertile imagination.

I purloined a sheet of the family notepaper, and in the privacy of the bathroom composed an epistle designed to melt a heart of stone. It went more or less as follows – though, for obvious reasons, I quote from memory.

Dear Miss Gray,

James [I thought that was a nice touch] is sorry that he annoyed you with his pistil and if you will give him it back again he promisses that he will never do it agen. (Signed) Mrs Dow.

I presented this first epistle of James to Miss Gray, who took rather a dim view of it. There must have been more subtle error in syntax which made her suspicious. She questioned me closely, but I stuck to my story. Finally she yielded and said that she had been going to return the revolver at four o'clock anyway. I may add that all the time I was being cross-examined I looked Miss Gray straight in the eye. Later in life I came to the conclusion that ability to do this is a prerequisite for the dedicated and successful liar.

But crows come home to roost. Ten years later, and after I had left school, I met Miss Gray on Lamlash golf course, of all places. After we had inquired kindly for each other's health and well-being she said: 'Jimmy, was that note from your mother?'

I confessed, and so got off my soul and conscience something that had not given them the slightest bother for the last ten years.

There was nothing in Class Five which sticks out in the memory. Possibly I was asleep most of the time. But Class Six was different. In Class Six I spent the most miserable year of my schooldays. Class Six was the 'Qualifying' class, and was an important one, since success in the 'Qually' opened the door to the Intermediate.

The teacher of Class Six shall be nameless, though a generation of Old Grammarians will remember her well. For some unknown reason she did not like me. I was different. I had about nineteen reasons for not liking her. She didn't like Johnnie either. Maybe because he was my friend. We had gone up school together like Tom Brown and Harry East. I simply could do nothing right for that woman. I won't labour the point, but will give one example which lingers in the mind.

It was customary for a class to give their teacher a present at Christmas, and for the last five years I had taken pleasure in asking Mother for the requisite threepence and handing it over to the treasurer *pro tem*. But this was different. Johnnie and I had a committee meeting.

There were our parents, we told one another, working their fingers to the bone to keep us in a fee-paying school. Was it fair that their hard-earned money should be handed out gratuitously to purchase a gift for a woman who was making our lives miserable? We blued the tanner. Johnnie, as far as I can remember, invested his threepence in Battleaxe toffee; he would get six bars. I bought a packet containing a dozen boxes of matches. We consumed the toffee up in the park, and watched the matches consuming themselves.

If ever I attain to being a saint, which, even if remotely possible, is highly unlikely, I will be honest when they come to canonize me. I will tell them that any pretensions I have to sanctity are due to the fact that early in life I concluded that I was plainly not cut out to be a sinner. I always got found out.

The little perisher who had organized the presentation did something not normally done. He bought a Christmas card to go along with the gift, and on it he wrote in his best penmanship (up light, down heavy) the names of the faithful who had contributed. You will no doubt remember Abou Ben Adhem, and how he asked the angel if his name was in the book? There was no point in Johnnie's or my doing any such thing. We knew our names were not there.

The gift was handed over. I do not know what it was. My mind was on other things. So apparently was Johnnie's, for he couldn't remember either. The teacher thanked the class, and then read the names on the card. She looked up. I had read somewhere of the Medusa whose glance turned men to stone. Johnnie and I would have made a pretty pair of statuary. Life can be very, very hard. It was in Class Six that for the only time I was sent to the Rector for punishment.

I had been given a geometry set, possibly to encourage me to get out of the 'Qually' and into the Intermediate. As if I needed any encouragement to get out of that class! I must have been toying with this geometry set when I should have been doing something else. The teacher came down like a wolf on the fold. She snatched the set from my hands and hurled it into a corner of the room. She then told me to pick it up. I refused.

I was like Sam who refused to pick up his musket until the Duke of Wellington asked him to. There was no Duke of Wellington in Class Six. He would not have lived five minutes with that woman. I was sent to the Rector.

George Aimer Russell, Rector of Paisley Grammar School, was a

B

gentlemanly type, as befitted one who was headmaster of the only Secondary school in the town. He was not addicted to belting, except on occasion, when the strength of one of the female teachers had given out. As my time and the Rector's were equally valuable, I did not, after I had knocked on his door and been summoned to the presence, beat about the bush. I pleaded guilty as charged, and George Aimer went over to the window and lowered the blinds, synchronizing with the lowering of my spirits.

This was the first time I had been in this position but more experienced criminals had told me that when George drew the blinds, you were for it. The Rector's room faced on to the Glasgow road, and any curious person with long sight or a telescope could see what was going on within. At that time hanging was done in private too.

Of course I did not mention this at home. Nowadays if a child gets belted, parents take a day off work and charge down to the school threatening the teacher with breach of the peace, habeas corpus, and assault and battery. Not in my day. This was a thing to keep dark, or you would have got another one to keep the first one company.

6. Much Reading . . .

Shortly after this we moved back to Mavisbank, as I think I have said, without giving any date, and for the first time I had my own room. We had been brought up to believe that the proper furnishing of any room is books.

I set up my bookcases, kindly donated by the grocer, and arranged my books. There were the prizes (all from the Sunday School, by the way). There were various other volumes that had come at Christmas and on birthdays, along with others that were taking up too much room in the house. I think Father must have been like myself who simply cannot throw out a book, no matter how long it is since I read it, and even though I have no intention of reading it again.

Father was a very bookish man, and so we all became as time went on. Brother Lex was particularly studious. He had started school ahead of me, but with various illnesses and a longer university courses – he took honours in history – I had caught up with him by the time we went to college.

Lex got a Military Cross serving with the Eighth Army in the desert, and rejoices (at least I hope he rejoices) in being a Doctor of Philosophy, a degree he received for writing a treatise on ministers of Scottish regiments.

Among our Christmas presents every year was the *Chums' Annual* for one of us and the *Boys' Own Annual* for the other. We read these avidly, though they were a bit heavy for reading in bed. In the normal way we went to bed fairly early but there were no real restrictions on how long you could read once you got there. We were allowed comics within reason, but these came out of pocket money.

There was *Chips* and *Comic Cuts*, Weary Willie and Tired Tim, Hector the Dog, and Waddles the Waiter, and the Casey Court Kids. Father would tell us of the comics of his day which, according to him, would have made Dracula look like a beginner. Their characters were Spring-heeled Jack, and a whole selection of vampires.

We had to be content with the more respectable stories contained in the *Union Jack* and other publications of the same kind, like the *Magnet*. Your pals got one and you got the other and you swopped over when you had read them. It was in the *Union Jack* that Sexton Blake was born. He lived to a ripe old age too, for he was a grown man when I first got to know him, and was still at the peak of his powers fifty years later. He started practice in 1894, which means that he's getting on a bit now. Tinker, his assistant, was much younger. He must be just a boy of around ninety.

All the detectives had the same kind of name as Sherlock Holmes: two syllables in the first name and one in the second. Nelson Lee was one, and Dixon Hawke was another.

The *Magnet* and the *Gem* produced the school stories, though to us a 'public school' was one where they didn't pay fees, But we read ravenously the stories of Greyfriars and St Jim's. Of course this had all started with *Tom Brown's Schooldays* and carried on with Talbot Baines Reed's books, like *The Fifth Form at St Dominic's*.

Sex, of course, was never mentioned in these stories. Some of the characters may have had sisters: Tom Merry, Frank Nugent, Harry Wharton, Hurree Jamset Singh and the others. But no sweethearts. Billy Bunter had a sister who appeared in some girls' magazine that was beneath our notice. Did you know that Billy Bunter's middle name was George?

It was, I think, in 1921 that the *Adventure* came on the scene, published in Dundee. I took it from the start. Each number had a coloured picture of a footballer. I wish I had them now. Later, from the same publisher, came the *Rover* and the *Wizard*. These, too, were really boys' papers. As far as they were concerned, Adam had never lost that rib. Of course the Wild West had its place too, and its prophet was Buffalo Bill.

I don't think modern comics are as good as the old ones, but maybe that's because I'm a boy no more. But you haven't read a book when the whole story is told in pictures. You ask a boy if he has read *Treasure Island* and he says that he has. But he hasn't. All he's done is look at pages of pictures with captions. His imagination has been given no exercise, and his vocabulary has not increased.

To digress again for a moment, I had a thought, when television began to show some of the 'classics' in serial form, that this was going to destroy reading completely. And I would certainly have appreciated a medium which made it unnecessary for me to read some of the classics prescribed for home reading. But the strange thing is that television has made these books more popular than ever they were before, to the delight of publishers who don't have to pay the author any royalties.

Apart from the books which were our own, there were plenty of others in the house, and we had access to them all, even to those in fine bindings. And at a very early age we joined Paisley's excellent public library.

I don't know how young I was when I first came on Poe's *Tales of Mystery and Imagination*, but I must have been well short of my teens. I loved it, especially *The Pit and the Pendulum*, and the one about the chap who was dying and who allowed himself to be hypnotized so that he stayed alive, and when they brought him round again he dissolved into a mass of corruption which made a terrible mess of the bed. They certainly never kept me off my sleep.

Of course if you want real horror there's not many books that can come up to Grimm's *Fairy Tales*, which is maybe why I always preferred them to Hans Andersen. After all, the story of Big Claus and Little Claus contains the destruction of five horses, one attempted murder and one successful murder. All good clean fun.

I was still pretty young, too, when I came on Jerome K. Jerome. It was *The Diary of a Pilgrimage* and I felt what Keats felt when he opened Chapman's Homer. A new planet had swum into my ken. It had me running to the library for the others, and never a year passes but I read *Three Men in a Boat* and find something new to laugh over every time. It is a very humbling exercise for one who tries to write humorous prose, for Jerome, like Thurber, is a master.

Scott I never could quite take to. He takes too long to get on with the job. They must have paid him by the line. But Dickens was different, especially *Pickwick Papers* and *Oliver Twist*. It's a great chapter where Bill Sikes murders Nancy.

Kipling's *Plain Tales from the Hills* was in the bookcase, and I began it a little uncertainly, but in no time I was under the spell of one of the great story-tellers of all time, though I did not appreciate this fully until much later I went to India as chaplain to the tea planters of South Sylhet, Assam. So it was Kipling from the library for a month or two. I have them all, and *Kim* is one of the bedside books.

Others I read as a boy and still read are Conan Doyle's *Sir Nigel* and *The White Company*. And, of course, Sherlock Holmes. I loved *The Speckled Band.* Professor Challenger at that time was appearing in the *Strand Magazine,* which Father brought home every month, and he was a favourite too. But a list of all the books I read would be far too long, and would be as incomplete as it would be tedious, and there is no particular moral in it.

One day I came on a book at home whose title appealed to me: it was *Self Help Smiles.* But there wasn't a smile, far less a laugh, in the first twenty pages. It was all about chaps who had got on in the world. Smiles was the author's name, and never was there a man with a less fitting one. My revulsion to this book may be one of the many reasons why I have not got on in the world.

And then I discovered Jeffery Farnol and fell in love with his heroines one after the other, though I always felt that I was being a little unfaithful to the last one by falling in love so readily with the next one. I felt that this touch of remorse was the least that I could do. Women, nowadays, describing anything from a hat to a sunset will call it 'gorgeous'. I reserve the word for Jeffery Farnol's heroines.

The reader may have noticed that so far there has been little or no reference to books which might be called 'elevating', and no reference at all to the Bible. But the Bible was part of our reading: it had to be, both in day school and Sunday School.

You got passages to learn: psalms, and parables, and the Ten Commandments, and the Sermon on the Mount, or parts of it. In day school you also had to learn the shorter catechism, which, I must confess, I have largely forgotten. Though there is nothing wrong with the shorter catechism. Most Scotsmen of an earlier day got their unique ability in theological argument from their intimate knowledge of 'The Carritches'. But in Sunday School there was also preparation for the Sunday School Union National Examination each year.

I always did pretty well in these examinations, and, if I remember aright, Lex won a Scottish silver medal one year. Years later I had to sit the entrance examination for Trinity College, and one of the papers is simply on knowledge of the scriptures. Men have been known to fail in this. I didn't fail, and one of the reasons was undoubtedly the store of knowledge I had acquired over the years, reading for the Sunday School Union examination.

Of course there was something superficial about this kind of thing. We were not dissecting and analysing, but we were at least getting a sound knowledge of what we were to dissect and analyse later. Which is a good way to get a start.

Kirk members very often complain that their minister isn't visiting enough. They would also complain if he came in the middle of *Coronation Street,* but there is no one more illogical than the kirk member. Unless it is the minister.

My session in Greenock once complained to me about this. Of course, they were not complaining that I wasn't working hard enough. It was just that I was spending more time in the parish among the unchurched than I was with the members. I didn't argue the point.

They insisted that in the old days Scots ministers spent a great deal of their time visiting the congregation. I conceded the point. I said further that I would follow the good example of the old-fashioned minister, and do the visiting as he did it. So I laid down the conditions.

I would publish, in the monthly news sheet which we distributed, the district which I would visit and the date of the visits. The elder of the district was to be with me. I expected the whole family to be present, except those who were working or at night school. I would examine the children to find how faithfully the parents were carrying out the baptismal vows by which they undertook, by precept and example, to raise their children in the nurture and admonition of the Lord. The visit would end with family prayers.

Enthusiasm for visitation thereafter waned, and the subject was not raised again. But this is, after all, what a pastoral visit was in the old days.

I may confess here and now that although I passed the college entrance examination in the English Bible, I failed in Hebrew. But that is something entirely different. Julius Caesar would have failed in Hebrew; so would Socrates. The thought has just struck me in the passing that they would have failed in the English Bible too. But I don't think there is any moral in that.

7. People Are People

When I think how pleasant life was in those early years (except for that year in Class Six) I cannot find it in my heart to envy the younger generation, and certainly not to wish that I were myself young again. This is not a very nice world to be young in. Or even to be old in. When folk say they would like to be young again they mean that they wish they could start over again with all their acquired knowledge (I do not use the word 'wisdom', since it is easier to acquire knowledge than it is to acquire wisdom). They would probably just make the same mistakes, though maybe in a different order.

A farthing was currency. With it you could buy a nailrod, which made a dosage of Gregory's mixture superfluous. You could get two liquorice straps, which you tore into thin strips like bootlaces to make them last longer. Or a soda lunch, which consisted of a container like a squib, filled with sherbet instead of gunpowder. Protruding from the top was a liquorice tube up which you sucked the sherbet until it became too wet because of the way your mouth watered. Along with it were two small biscuits the like of which I have never seen since soda lunches went out.

For the price you paid for a bar of toffee you would be lucky today to get a couple of aspirins. I forget what a loaf cost, but it was something with an odd three farthings. You got a choice. You could either take the farthing or a couple of tapers.

Paisley, unlike Greenock, is a town without an east end and a west end. Geographically there is one of each, of course, but socially there is not. Or at least there was not when we lived there. 'Toney' parts and 'untoney' parts there were, naturally, but they were mixed up all over the burgh, not concentrated in one place. Greenock, unlike Jerusalem, and even unlike Paisley, is not compactly built together, for the available building land was the narrow coastal strip between the Clyde and the hills.

Greenlaw Avenue was in the east of Paisley, Mavisbank was in the south-west, but both were the good, honest, substantial tenements in which lived and no doubt still live, the solid middle-class families who were, and are, the long-suffering backbone of the country. But to get to Mavisbank from the centre of the town you had to pass through a really slummy part: the Saucel, where there were always blowsy women and boozey men, and rickety children hanging about the close mouths. Even as a boy this used to annoy me. Not because I had to pass these people four times a day on my way to and from school, and twice on Sundays for a bonus. What annoyed me was that Society, or what I understood by Society, should allow these conditions to exist at all.

Father was a Liberal. Paisley was Liberal to the core, though it was changing even then. But I was beginning to realize that in the Liberalism of that day there was a basic weakness. It was *laissez-faire*, 'let be'. You must not interfere with the freedoms of other people. If they wanted to make a kirk or a mill of it, that was their affair. I'm still a Liberal, and if I can't remain one out of principle I'll remain one out of spite and keep living to see the day when they change their name and become the Radical Party, and put the other two in their places.

I remember Father saying one Sunday as we were passing the Saucel something that was not at all like him. I resented it.

There was a young woman leaning against the wall. It's almost impossible to describe her in mere English. She was shachly, she was bauchly, and her wean was peelie-wallie. The words are self-explanatory. Father said, 'The sins of the fathers are visited on the children.'

As I have said, this was not like him. He was devoting a good deal of his time to trying to do something for people like that. Later on I had some words with God about this, for God and I have been on very familiar terms for a long time now. I told God, plump, plain, and proper, that if He had anything to do with creating the Saucel, He and I had come to the parting of the ways. God assured me that He had nothing to do with it, and I took His word for it.

But this must have gone down into my subconscious, and maybe it was then and there that the germ of the idea was born, that if I couldn't do anything about the Saucel and if God couldn't do anything about the Saucel – this Saucel and all the other Saucels – there might be a chance that God and I could do it between us, or at least make a start. But some years were to pass before that thought really became conscious.

What I wanted to know, though I don't think I ever asked, was why the churches didn't do more about it than they did. St James' church was one of the affluent ones, with some of the Coats family occupying the back pew, which, as all the world knew in the days of seat rents, were the most expensive sittings. And thither we walked every Sunday, past the far from pellucid river Cart, which was little more than an open sewer, up Oakshaw and down the Stoneybrae. About a mile and a half it would be, I suppose. Me in that detested kilt, which was usually greeted at the Saucel by facetious remarks and rude songs, one of which stated crudely that in the philabeg my posterior must be frozen.

It wasn't that Father objected to Sunday transport; it was just that there was none going in our direction. There were no buses at all, just the tram-cars, which didn't suit.

They can say what they like about the churches losing their grip on the so-called working class, but in my experience, which is rather more considerable than most, the churches never had any grip. The churches were in the main middle class, though it is always dangerous to generalize.

The middle class have come in for a good deal of criticism, and much of it in the old days was deserved, but they had their good points too. Of course the corporations of the burghs were made up mainly of middle-class men, and since they owned or rented houses of fair size, and operated businesses, it was obviously in their own interest to keep the rates as low as possible, with the result that many Scottish towns lacked amenities, which were really necessities. These are now being provided at vast cost, for which future generations will have to pay.

Greenock talked about public baths for a hundred years (this is fact, not exaggeration) before they were built. And they haven't been built all that long. With a few honourable exceptions, the big industrialists of the Lower Reaches have left no monument of this kind behind them. Paisley was different. Old Sir Thomas Glen Coats once said that Paisley made the Coats and the Coats made Paisley.

There were also the Clarks and others, who spent their money in the town and on the town, and it was money well spent.

On the whole I would say that the much maligned middle class of yesterday were much more generous proportionately than are the gainfully employed today, who, if they gave as generously as the others gave, would save the churches much financial headache.

Many of the middle-class churches supported missions in the poorer areas of the town, and the disappearance of these missions has been not entirely a good thing, though there may have been a certain patronizing element about them, and a persuasion that a moral obligation can be fulfilled simply by gifts of money. But it was in these missions that the Band of Hope flourished, and the Foundry-boys and the Penny Savings Bank. This is where the Boys' Brigade began.

And this, by and large, was the pattern of St James' morning Sunday School, which we attended, and as a result I was brought in touch at an early and impressionable age with boys and girls, and with Sunday School teachers, who lived in circumstances rather different from those I was being brought up in. The result is that I spent a large part of my subsequent ministry in the East End, apart from five years in India, and the last seven years in the island of Arran. I was getting past the stair-climbing exercise by then. I liked these people, and I think, without being immodest, that they liked me.

Mind you, if I said that I would never have done in a West End church, that would be a form of inverted snobbery. Like the chap who says: 'Of course, I'm only a working man . . .'

To do good work in the ministry a man has to be happy. And the first thing he has to do, after he has assessed his possibilities, is to assess his limitations. If more did this in every trade and profession there would be fewer square pegs in round holes, and fewer men toiling away and longing for the day when they will retire and start living.

But I wouldn't insult my Glasgow congregation or my Greenock congregation by giving the impression that they were people of the slums. They were anything but. Parts of the parishes were pretty slummy, though. But a slum isn't houses, it's people. Mrs McDade lived in what could be called a slum.

Mrs McDade was our washing machine when I was a boy.

8. Mrs McDade

Disputation about whose turn it was for the washing-house key is not unknown in the tenements of Scotland. But not in highly respectable Greenlaw Avenue or Mavisbank Terrace.

There were six houses in the block and since no one would have dreamed of doing the washing on a Saturday, far less on a Sunday, there must have been some arrangement covering the five remaining days. What it was, I do not know. But there was never any trouble.

The washing house was down the back stairs from the close. On one side were the six cellars, and, on the other, the wash-house with its two wooden tubs and the cast-iron boiler. When it was Mother's turn you were sent down first thing in the morning to light the boiler fire, being well warned to fill the boiler first with water. Mrs McDade arrived a little later for her breakfast.

It was a great and respectable thing to hang out a good washing, and Mother maintained that there was a woman in the next close who hung out the same one every week. Of course you did your best to keep out of your mother's way on washing day, when her temper was liable to become a little frayed at the edges, especially if the rain came on just when the things were nearly dry.

Mrs McDade was of an indeterminate age, but certainly not young. She was as Irish as the mountains of Mourne, and her instrument was the washing board, which at that time had not achieved musical status.

If it was during the school holidays I might help her by tramping the blankets. I don't know what it did for the blankets, but it was certainly good for the feet. The soap powder was Isdale and McCallum's, and sixty years ago each packet of A1 soap powder contained a coupon. You could gather these up and exchange them for gifts at the works, which were, of course, in Paisley. There is nothing new under the sun.

Mrs McDade lived in a poor street off the Glasgow road, and if Mother wanted her specially for anything I would take a message to her on my way to school. She would ask me in and give me a piece and a penny. Poor soul. she hadn't many pennies. I don't suppose she would get much more than a half-crown for her day's washing, with her meals thrown in, of course. The meals were important.

Her hands fascinated me. They were more like claws than hands, bleached from years of washing other people's clothes. These hands were all she had. She had more reason to insure them than Paderewski had. She sat with the family at the kitchen table on washing day. Father never came home for lunch on washing day. I used to wonder why. Now I know. It had nothing to do with Mrs McDade. It must have had something to do with Mother.

Mrs McDade's manipulation of a knife was something that had to be seen to be believed. Nothing ever fell off it. Not even peas. My dinner would get cold while I watched her, for I was perfectly certain that at one point she would cut her throat from the inside. One Friday we had mince.

Mrs McDade, who was a Roman Catholic, was fairly enjoying it. Mince sits nicely on a knife and does not really demand the presence of teeth. Mrs McDade had only two and they weren't opposite one another. Then Mother said: 'Oh, Mrs McDade, I'm sorry. I forgot it was Friday.'

The poor old soul laid down her knife and pushed the plate away. There may well have been a tear in her eye. She said, 'God forgive ye, Mistress Dow, but why did ye remind me?'

Nothing would persuade her to carry on with the mince, and Mother made her scrambled egg. But what is scrambled egg compared with mince?

This was my first encounter with the other religion, since no Roman Catholics lived in Mavisbank. I was aware that there was a difference, for we had Roman Catholics in school. But the only difference between them and us was that they didn't come in to morning prayers, but got on with their homework.

Though reference to mince reminds me of a time when I asked Mother if they had mince and potatoes and peas in heaven. Good woman that she was, she said she didn't think so. My notion of Paradise took a severe blow from which it has not fully recovered.

I always treated Mrs McDade with complete respect, and would have been in trouble if I had not. She was the first of many fine folk of the same sort that I was to know, and respect, and even love in the years to come.

9. Family Audience

There was, of course, a street football team and a street cricket team, according to the season. Before the season opened we went round the doors soliciting subscriptions and always got enough for replacement of gear. We trained in the washhouse of number eleven and by going runs out the Barrhead road. We did this so faithfully that when it came to playing a match we were exhausted. Somebody got a recipe for embrocation and we clubbed together and bought the ingredients. I seem to remember turpentine and wintergreen. We stank to high heaven. Sometimes we broke training and smoked.

The first thing I smoked as a little lad was rolled-up brown paper. I do not recommend it, for it is quite unsatisfactory. You can't cough properly for being sick and you can't be sick properly for coughing. Its sole merit was cheapness and availability. From this we graduated to cinnamon stick, which you bought in the chemist's if you had any money. The chemist must have known what you wanted it for. I never heard of cinnamon stick being used for anything else. Maybe he thought it was to cure a chest trouble, for which mothers used to take their offspring to the vicinity of a tarry boiler.

Tea was quite satisfactory too, and was always procurable, since most homes have some. You smoked it in a wee pipe with a red bowl like a cherry. Before going to Assam I hadn't smelled burning tea for years. But the minute I put my head into the factory where the green tea was being dried, my mind went back, and my stomach turned over nostalgically.

Tobacco was occasionally accessible too, for Father smoked a pipe, and a cigar on high days and holidays, including communion Sunday. He must have felt that a cigar went better with his tile hat. But the trouble with pipe tobacco is that the mixture which doesn't choke you burns your tongue, and the mixture which doesn't burn your tongue chokes you.

On the whole I would offer this advice to any boy who thinks of taking up smoking: remember that after Old King Cole had sent for his pipe he sent for his bowl.

Before we joined the Scouts we would wait at teatime on a Friday to see if Father took off his boots. We had no fear of him going on the skyte on a Friday night or any other night for that matter. But if he kept his boots on we knew we were going to the pictures. There were a fair number of places of entertainment in Paisley, and all well enough patronized.

There was the Picture House on the High Street, which was later joined by the Palace. There was the Rink, which at one time had been a roller-skating rink, and the Royal Animated, later known as the Glen Cinema, and the scene of the terrible disaster one New Year.

During the War (the First War, that is) there were pictures shown in the Town Hall. This was the Clark Cinema. You got a vocalist thrown in, though some of them would have been better thrown out. They would sing 'There's a long, long trail a-winding', and we would all sing 'Keep the home fires burning', though the reason half the audience were there was that they didn't have any coal at home.

The Rink programme was half film and half variety. The lower classes sat in front and the upper classes sat behind a barrier at the back. The Dows were upper class. There was only one projector, which meant that there were several hiatuses in the programme. The screen would go suddenly bright, till they put on a slide which said that was the end of part one, and that part two would follow immediately.

The Royal Animated was well named, which brings me to another digression.

If ever I should be asked to nominate the recipient of the Nobel Peace Prize I would unhesitatingly say: 'The chap who invented DDT.' Any social worker of around my age would assuredly subscribe to that. He might even subscribe to the prize.

There are certain people who have a peculiar attraction for fleas. I am one of them. There may be something in my blood, I do not know. But fleas have had a fair sample of it. I could no more keep away from them than they could keep away from me.

I got them even on a Sunday, and there is fair scope for a flea when a chap is wearing a kilt. They murdered me.

You never see a flea these days; and I speak with authority, for if there was a flea within a mile of me it would reach me by leaps and bounds. On a Friday night when the word got around that Father hadn't taken off his boots, all the fleas in Paisley would foregather at the Rink. If the Dows did not turn up they would jump on a green tram-car and head for Paisley Cross and the Animated. They would then send out scouts to see if we had maybe bypassed the Animated and gone to the Picture House.

As far as the films themselves were concerned there would always be a serial involving Ruth Roland or Pearl White, and it always stopped when she was tied to the line and the train was approaching, or when she was fast approaching the attentions of a circular saw. But she was always there next week.

The cowboy hero was Big Bill Hart. Everybody thought he was a baddie until his heart was touched by a dear old lady or a little girl with golden hair. This brought out the best in him, and he would expire (taking some time to do so) surrounded by the weeping people who had misjudged him. I don't suppose any hero died more regularly than Big Bill Hart did.

The Keystone Cops had us rolling in the aisles, and can still have this effect on me. As far as I am concerned, I am a lowbrow of the lowest sort. I used to embarrass my fiancée, when I acquired one, by applauding when the Three Stooges came on.

There was, of course, Charlie Chaplin, and Buster Keaton, and Chester Conklin and Slim Summerville, and Fatty Arbuckle, and rare Ben Turpin. When they show old films on TV I always like to be in the company of small boys. It's a great comfort to know that they enjoy them still as much as I did.

Then there were the cartoons; and the first character I remember was Felix the Cat, followed by Mickey Mouse and Popeye. About the only cartoon that's done better nowadays is *Tom and Jerry*. If I lived in the constituency of that MP who wanted *Tom and Jerry* banned on grounds of violence, he would never get a vote from me.

We lost our young hearts to Marie Prevost, and Phyllis Haver, Mabel Norman, and later, of course, to Mary Pickford and Clara Bow. Up in Kilpatrick's stable across the Park we did the athletic things that Douglas Fairbanks (Senior, of course) did, and wee Nicholson broke his leg when we were sliding down the chute which conveyed the hay from the loft to the ground floor. Wull the carter had removed it for the horse's tea just as wee Nicholson was on his way.

There were no Westerns: there were just cowboy pictures, with the cowboys wearing *chaparejos* that looked as if they had been made out of discarded hearthrugs bought at a jumble sale in Dodge City. One thing that was never allowed in a cowboy picture was for the hero to kiss the heroine, or any other woman for that matter. Hoot Gibson did not do it, nor did Tom Mix. They just rode away together into the black and white sunset. What they did after that was nobody's business but their own.

A white-haired mother might implant a juicy one on the forehead of her son before he rode away to hold up another bank, but that was the limit. Cowboy pictures have deteriorated since they started giving Oscars for osculation. Nowadays the chap can't get on with the business of killing the baddies, for kissing the lassies.

Father was very fond of the theatre, and the songs he would sing to infant Elsie were the great songs of the variety stage, which still survive. Just like the old Redemption hymns, to which they are closely related.

But the old theatres are gone, which is a great pity, for I have a notion that the demand for them will come back. Your great singers and comedians served their time in wee theatres in the towns of Scotland. Harry Lauder started with the Glasgow 'Bursts'. Will Fyffe and the other 'greats' like Tommy Lorne and George West learned their trade, and how to deal with refractory audiences, in the wee smoke-filled, low-roofed, riotous places of entertainment which you would find in every sizable town in the land. I first met Jimmy Logan when the family were playing the Greenock Empire, which, like the rest of them, is now no more. Many a good night we had in the Paisley theatre which, too, has gone with the wind of change.

There was Dr Walford Bodie, whose speciality was electricity, which was largely a mystery to the majority whose houses were lit by gas. He would invite unsuspecting members of the audience to join him on the stage, and would then pass electric currents through them to the great delight of those who had decided not to join him on the stage. He was a very good conjurer too.

Paisley's main egg dealer was 'Egg' Noble. Dr Bodie had a trick by which he turned an egg into a hen. It was a trick nearly as clever as nature's way of doing the same thing. But more sensational. It was also quicker. 'Egg' Noble challenged Dr Bodie to do the trick with one of Noble's eggs. This inspired a certain amount of low wit, which I will not go into in detail, since the firm, I believe, is still in existence. Though not, I presume, with the same eggs.

On the night of the challenge the theatre was packed from floor to ceiling, but Bodie did it. Everyone was amazed, especially those who thought that Bodie had a special egg stuffed with hens.

Chung Ling Soo was another great conjurer who appeared in the Paisley Hippodrome. In one of his tricks his wife fired shots at him and he caught the bullets on a plate. Something went wrong with the rifle one night, and he was shot and killed on the stage.

The winter had two highlights: Hengler's Circus, and the Princess Pantomime. Doodles was the clown at Hengler's, and the show always finished with the water scene. The floor of the ring went down and was flooded with water. There would be a waterfall pouring down from the roof, with a bridge across it so that the stage-coach could thunder over pursued by the Indians.

If I mention the artistes of the old days, somebody is sure to write and say that So-and-so didn't appear at the Princess, but at the Theatre Royal, or the King's, or the Empress, or somewhere else. My memory isn't as accurate as all that. But we saw them all: Jack Anthony, Tommy Lorne, Dave Willis, Harry Gordon, Tommy Morgan, and the one I count the greatest of all, Will Fyffe.

In the pantomimes there was never the faintest trace of suggestiveness – though I wouldn't have known what suggestiveness was. The humour was broad, but all good humour is broad. The Dame never pretended to be anything but a man dressed up as a woman. Who could ever have taken Tommy Lorne for a woman? Then a new school of thought appeared. I suppose George Lacey would be the first Dame who tried to look like a woman. If so, he has an awful sin to answer for. Others followed, including Harry Gordon; and something was lost.

In the same way, nobody ever would have thought that the

Principal Boy was a man. Dorothy Ward is the one I remember best. She had legs like Marlene Dietrich only she had more of them. I don't mean that she had three legs, but the two she had were more substantial.

In the summer the artistes all departed for the coast. In Rothesay you always had Charlie Kemble and Billy Oswald. Nobody of my time will ever forget Charlie's wee song which he made up on the stage as he went along. At least that was the impression he gave, and that is the mark of the true artist.

On the serious side we saw and heard Brandon Thomas, and the O'Mara Opera Company, and D'Oyly Carte. We saw Benson, and Martin Harvey, and Matheson Lang in *The Wandering Jew,* and Gielgud in *King Lear*.

Martin Harvey was an Old Grammarian. I don't know how many Old Grammarians know this, but it is true. I discovered this when, in the year after I left school, we decided to found the Paisley Grammar Former Pupils Rugby Team. I was appointed its first secretary. I don't know how many they have had since, but I am sure they never had a worse one.

A properly constituted club must have an honorary president, and vice-presidents, and others who will be good for a subscription. Careful inquiries were made and we ascertained that the Astronomer Royal, by the name of Jackson, was an Old Grammarian, and so was Sir John Martin Harvey. I was instructed to write to him, offering him the distinction of being the first honorary vice-president of the club, which is now approaching its jubilee.

He accepted, but he either forgot to enclose the cheque or he remembered not to. It was a far, far, worse thing he did than he had ever done.

10. Listeners In

We must have been among the first in Paisley to have a wireless set. I still have the original licence. The number is A 10058, and the date of issue is 23 March 1923, which makes me just fifteen. Father was very attached to that set. Of course, to hear anything at all you had to be attached to the set, for it was a headphone job. If you forgot you had them on and stood up, there was trouble.

The aerial went down from the kitchen window, three storeys up, to a pole in the back green, with china insulators that would not have been out of place at Dounreay. There was also an earth wire which went by a devious route to the water pipe of the closet cistern.

Why they ever called these things 'wireless' sets I have never understood. Our set seemed to be all wires. And yet, when you come to think of it, the younger generation take the transistor set for granted. But even the transistor set needs a battery. The old crystal set needed no such adventitious or artificial aids. All you needed was the crystal, and the cat's whisker, whatever was inside the box, the earphones, and a certain amount of faith.

Lex and I got the aerial rigged up in the afternoon, to the tremendous interest of the other residents in the Terrace, and at teatime Father came in with the set. It had cost him, if I remember aright, about seven pounds ten, which would be about a week's salary. The monetary cost of what was inside it I do not know, but apart from the french-polished box in which the internals reposed, I would think the total value of the thing would be around fifteen bob.

Father followed the directions carefully, and fitted the thing up. He fiddled with the cat's whisker, with a wrapt expression on his face and his mouth slightly open; which, as all the world knows, is a great help to hearing. Sounds came through.

We all stood in a queue, waiting for our turn with the headphones, without which you could hear nothing. We watched with amazement the expressions on the faces of the other members of the family who had been elected to precede us. I don't know what the others got, but, when it came my turn, I got 'The Ride of the Valkyries' out of *Die Walküre*. If that was the race they rode in.

After this introduction the novelty wore off; except for Father, who was devoted to the thing. He could hardly finish his tea before he had the headphones clamped on. Then there would come a night when the old man, after much open-mouthed manoeuvring, had managed to get the cat's whisker placed on the point of the crystal which was giving perfect reception, and Mother would poke the fire. He would thereupon get on to her for disturbing what he recognized to be a scientific experiment, and she would ask him if the fire was to go out to let him play with his toys.

In due time we would be sent off to bed, and Father could then get down to uninterrupted listening for another couple of hours. It would be a play, or something of the sort, which required a dramatic end, or climax. Father would be waiting for this, all agog, and Mother, who was rather bored with the whole business, and who had put on the other pair of headphones only to keep Father company, would be waiting for this dénouement. Then one of the three of us would feel the call of nature, get up, and head for the bathroom.

Being well brought up, we always pulled the chain. Ours was not one of these modern gallon-and-a-half cisterns, which have been made necessary since more and more houses have been provided with all mod. cons. Ours was one that would have warmed the heart of Archimedes, or even cooled his ardour. When you pulled the chain it was like the Falls of Tummel in spate. I don't think Father ever heard that climax. I don't think that Mother minded a great deal.

One night Father came home with an air of mystery and a copy of the now defunct *Weekly Herald*, which, at that time, specialized in do-it-yourself wireless sets. It contained the first diagrams and instructions for the building of something called the PPV 2. Father asked me if I could follow the directions and build this two-valve set. He would pay for the components. I agreed. I know why I agreed. I didn't want to disappoint the old man. Why he should ever have asked me to have a bash at it I do not know to this day. Maybe he thought that with wireless telegraphy in its infancy, I might one day make a living out of it, since in his opinion I was obviously incapable of making a living by more conventional methods. Maybe he had no such thoughts.

I have not proved unable to make an honest living. But I proved, there and then, that I was physically and mentally incapable of making a living by building wireless sets.

I can remember what that set looked like. I cannot remember what it sounded like, for it never uttered a single sound. That this was not the fault of the designer I will freely admit. But at this time I was receiving a classical education which dealt with manners and modes that had never heard of Marconi, news being conveyed from Marathon and other places by runner. Father was not happy about the progress of James' PPV 2.

He would come home at teatime and tell me that he had been speaking to this chap while they were drinking coffee instead of getting on with their work, and this chap had told him that his six-year-old son, without any help, had built a PPV 2, and that they could get Paris. I would tell Father that I didn't believe his friend, and that, furthermore, Paris was no place for a six-year-old boy to be listening in to, and that it was no place for an elder of the church to be listening in to. Especially one who was also a Sunday School superintendent.

Finally Father got a friend to make him a valve set, and I was so hurt that I never listened to it, but went upstairs and got on with my work. Which is probably one of the reasons why I have done rather well off radio and television with the passing years.

11. Rooms with Attendance

We usually had two holidays in the year: a fortnight in the spring and a month in the summer. Father, of course, had only the usual summer fortnight, but in the spring we would settle somewhere handy that he could travel to: places like Largs, or Dunoon, Millport, or Port Bannatyne. Even Gourock, which is accounted a holiday resort by anyone who doesn't come from Greenock.

One year when we were on holiday at Port Bannatyne, Grandfather died. He had been on holiday with us. He would be in his early sixties. The authorities were most distressed about this.

They were not distressed that Grandfather had died. Just that he had been so uncooperative as to die on the island of Bute, where they were so proud of their vital statistics. I am now a councillor of Buteshire, and I have never forgiven them for their attitude to Grandfather. It was the first time I had been in the presence of death. I would be nine or ten years old. It didn't impress me.

We took his body back to Dundee to be buried, and I felt very proud when four members of the crew, in their dark blue jerseys, shouldered the coffin and carried it down the pier, and the flag was lowered to half-mast. This was my grandfather, and I thought it was the least they could do.

His father had sailed his own coaster out of Dundee, and he had a brother Tom, whom I never knew. There were two velvet waistcoats in our house that had once belonged to Father's Uncle Tom, who was, according to Father, the Casanova of Dundee. It is possible that I may have more relatives than appear on the family tree.

Father had one aunt living at that time, Aunt Mary, and it was from her house that Grandfather's funeral took place. It was the first funeral I had attended, and was to be the last until Father died in 1927. I must have attended at least two thousand since.

We went to Largs several times for the spring holidays. The house was on the front, the close next to the Moorings, though there were no Moorings then. It was up a red cammed stair with the closet on the landing. And the landlady was a bit of a tartar, though a very good cook.

During the holiday I fell off the Esplanade and twisted my knee. The family said it was a pity I hadn't fallen on my head and so suffered no damage. One afternoon the family went out to do something athletic, like putting, which was becoming very popular with non-golfers, and left me to my convalescence with my foot up on a chair. The landlady came in and asked me if my knee was getting better. I said it was coming on fine. Wherewith she removed my foot from its rest and set it on the floor with the remark that in that case there was no need for me to have it on her good chair.

It's a pity when this is all that you can remember about a person after all these years. She wasn't like old Dugald, who shelled mussels at Wilson's slip at Port Bannatyne, though she was probably a far better kirk attender, and therefore a far better 'Christian' than Dugald was. Dugald liked wee boys. Nobody else believed his stories. Indeed, nobody else listened to them, having heard them already when they were wee boys. Dugald had been captain of the royal yacht.

The number of ancient mariners I have met who had been captain or at least first mate of the royal yacht I do not know. Nor do I know how they accommodated all of them. I don't think you could have got a job as galley boy without an extra master's certificate. When Dugald was shelling mussels for bait he would have a faraway look in his eyes. He would be looking at the world's far horizons, and seeing, like John Masefield, strange lands from under the arched white sails of ships. I don't know how many boats he had been on. He must have been on at least one, since Bute is an island. Unless, of course, he was born on Bute.

But I'll never forget Dugald for one thing. We went out drowing for lythe, for I was a fair oarsman even as a little lad. He got into a beauty. He bade me ship the oars and come down to the stern. He handed me the rod, and said: 'He's your fish, Jimmy.' It's great when after all these years this is what you remember about somebody. Wherever you are, Dugald, if you don't tell St Peter about that fish, I will when I arrive.

Afterwards, Lamlash on the island of Arran became our place of summer holiday. Arran is an island that you either love or loathe. There is nothing in between. We loved it, though I never thought I would be a minister on it. Least of all at Lochranza.

One year when I would be about fourteen we switched our loyalty from Lamlash to Lochranza and spent a thoroughly miserable month of August. It rained all the time, and we thought the people, both natives and visitors, very snooty. Most of the visitors to Lochranza came from Greenock, for there was a direct sailing. There were no buses on the island in those days and almost no cars. You went to a place and there you stayed until the next boat came in.

Years and years later I went to Greenock, and met the folk who had been boys when I was a boy and who had been on holiday when I was on holiday at Lochranza. And I had thought they were snooty, and no doubt they had thought that I was snooty. And they weren't that way at all, and neither was I. Which just goes to show how fallible is human judgement. But we decided that next year it would be Lamlash once more. Lochranza had had it. I've been here since 1965.

Sanitation in Arran in those days was a bit primitive, though one old chap said to me years later that there hadn't been a decent leek grown on Arran since they brought in 'thae damn water closets'.

It was at Lamlash that I first played the game of bowls. This would be around the age of fifteen. Paisley always played Kilmarnock at Lamlash, for Paisley Fair and Kilmarnock Fair fell in the first fortnight of August. My friend George and I played most mornings and we were selected for the Paisley team, who must have been two short. We've been playing the game more or less ever since, and George skipped the Cardonald rink which won the Scottish rinks at Queen's Park a year or two ago. I never quite attained that far, though I have my trophies. George, who built a house in Lochranza and who became my organist, died suddenly in 1972.

'Letting' houses on Arran are hard to come by these days. When houses fall vacant they are snapped up at ridiculous prices by mainland folk who want a summer house. But this is changing too. More and more are trying to get away from the mainland rat-race, take their retirement as early as possible, or a golden handshake if one is proffered, and come down here and start to live. And those who have come to my parish are very good members of the kirk, though they were originally of all sorts of denominations. In fact they're keener on the kirk than many of the locals are.

In the old days, however, there were plenty of houses to let for the summer, either with or without attendance. Mother insisted that a house without attendance was just a change of sink. I don't know what Father thought, but we always had a house with attendance.

And, of course, where you have a house with attendance you have a landlady. Otherwise there wouldn't be any attendance. But with the departure of the letting house the landlady has largely become a person of the past. I think that this is a pity. Take tourism, for example, which is now one of Scotland's main industries. Mind you, I don't know that I'm all too keen on this, for I wouldn't like Scotland to become a country of obsequious waiters. We've got to bring back the coast landlady, for she was never obsequious.

I throw this idea out gratuitously to the Scottish Tourist Board, who may well throw it back. But if we seriously want to increase tourism in Scotland, and especially around the old towns of the Firth of Clyde, our best bet is to recapture the image of the landlady. They have schools for learning hotel management. Why not a school for the training of a new generation of landladies?

When they advertise Scotland's attractions they put the emphasis on the wrong things (apart from the scenery and the fishing, and the items we have which were there before tourism attracted Doctor Samuel Johnson). They don't think of anything better than making hotels bigger, higher and plushier, with more chromium plate and tartan wallpaper and carpets. I always feel that people should take their shoes off before they walk over a carpet of my tartan, which is a very popular one for carpets, being the Buchanan, or 'bum-bee', tartan. They want more background pop music, and more french-polished Italian head waiters, born and reared in places like Port Glasgow. And all that kind of thing.

But it doesn't matter how much plush, and chromium, and head waiters, and height and width you have, you will never have as much or as many as the Americans have at home. You can have more and more mod. cons., but you won't make them any modder or more convenient than they enjoy back home in the States. Or say that they enjoy.

They know all about this kind of thing. What they do not know about is the Scots landlady. They do not know, for they have never met her. She is not there to be met. It is time she was.

Suppose you have a millionaire from Milwaukee who has been going round Scotland from one plushy hotel to another. Finally he gets back home and is asked by the local Chamber of Commerce to give them a lecture on darkest Scotland and the Way Out. He wouldn't have a single thing to say that would be of the slightest interest to anyone. He could tell them that here and there he was overcharged in a Scots accent, instead of in a French accent, or a Spanish accent, or even in an American accent. But this does not make his wanderings unique, or lecturable. His fellow Rotarians know all about this, for they, too, have suffered.

But think what this chap could tell them if he had taken his nearest and dearest to Scottish rooms with attendance. Anywhere from Maidenkirk to John o' Groats.

He could hold his audience in the hollow of his hand. He could play on their emotions as on a ten-stringed instrument, which was known to the Psalmist before pop singers were invented. He could hold them, like the Ancient Mariner, saying: 'There was a house!'

He could tell them of the red-cammed spiral staircase at the end of the close, with the wee door on the landing that could not be entered unless the person who wanted to use the facilities was in possession of the key with the bobbin attached to it, which hung conveniently from a hook in the lobby. Had it been hung from a hook in the kitchen, it would have been embarrassing. When anyone removed it, everybody would have known where he or she was going.

Our American could tell his friends of how he had skinned his shins crawling over the board which protects the box-bed, and how he skinned them another couple of times because he had forgotten to turn off the gas before he departed to his slumbers. He could tell of the breath-taking view of the sea, seen between two chimneys of the house across the street: of the front room with the horsehair chairs. They don't have them today because there are so few horses. And the table covering, with the pom-poms.

He would describe the brass pot with the aspidistra, and the over-mantel with the china ornaments, gathered from the ends of the earth: places like Oban, and Campbeltown and Carnoustie. Cups and saucers, and sauce boats, and things with sticky-out bits for holding diamond rings, and things with no sticky-out bits for holding false teeth. Each one with the coat of arms of the town of its origin. If some of the children broke one, the landlady would tell you that no amount of money could compensate for its destruction. But your mother was expected to try.

There would be the marble time-piece, presented to the land-lady's husband on the occasion of his retirement from the cleansing service in 1904, since when it hasn't gone. He probably died in self-defence.

This American would have something of real interest and signi-ficance to report to his fellows, who would troop over in their thou-sands to discover if all this was true. Where others have been living on the outskirts of Scottish geography, this chap has been living in the intimacies of Scottish history.

Here's an American who has been plugging in an electric shaver ever since the first manly down appeared on his sallow cheeks. He has never fallen over a copper can of hot water left by a land-lady at the bedroom door. The reason why he should fall over it is that, equipped with the key with the bobbin, he is trying to get to the wee room on the landing before the man across the landing makes it.

He is used to a hotel bedroom with a bath. But this is not a change for him; and a holiday, above everything else, must surely be a change. Give him a wooden washstand, with a marble top, cracked across the middle, and a ewer and basin to match the third recep-tacle, kept in decent obscurity in the wee press down below, and which is to be used only when the weather is too cold to venture forth down the stairs with the key with the bobbin.

The bedstead will be of brass, with no knobs on the ends of the bedposts, these having been exported to America years before, and now worn round the neck of the wife on a platinum chain.

And the meals! This is where the real novelty would come in. What new experience is it for an American tourist to sit in a shiny grill room, with a fitted carpet, and soft music playing, ordering a mixed grill in bad French from an Italian waiter whose grandfather had a chip shop in Lesmahagow?

One mixed grill is the same as another mixed grill, except that some are more mixed and others are less grilled. One plate of soup tastes exactly the same as another plate of soup out of a similar packet. But this is not true of the meals provided by a landlady in rooms with attendance.

There will be for breakfast the simple plate of porridge, generously served so that you will not be inclined to ask for a second egg. When the egg arrives it may be consumed in one of two ways: eaten with a pick or sucked up through a straw. The toast is served in a rack. When you lift one slice you lift the lot. Then the rack falls off and breaks the cup. Along with the pot of tea, there is placed on the table a pot of hot water. Why this should be, nobody has ever discovered, since there is no threat to the nerves in the original infusion.

There are home-made scones from the Co-operative, and marmalade in a pot with the golliwog steamed off. For lunch on Sunday the main dish is hot roast mutton. On Monday cold roast mutton, followed by stovies on Tuesday and shepherd's pie on Wednesday. On Thursday and Friday she will go off meat altogether, serving sausages on the Thursday and fish on the Friday, in case the guest happens to be Roman Catholic.

Of course things have changed since I was a boy: habits, prices, menus, and even, possibly, the sheets, but I am convinced that if we are to attract visitors to these shores we will have to rediscover, or, if necessary, to resurrect, the coast landlady in her tight black blouse, with her hair done up in a bun at the back.

12. A Little Learning

One of the common complaints of middle-aged Clydesiders is the disappearance of the old passenger boats of grace and beauty, and their replacement by car ferries which have neither. There are few who have had as intimate a connection with Clyde passenger boats as I have. It occurred during one Easter holiday when we were living in Gourock.

In Cardwell Bay was a boat hirer who had one vessel equipped with a lugsail. It was my ambition to sail this boat. I went down to the slip at about eight in the morning, to be sure that I was first in the queue. The man asked me if I was familiar with lugsails. I endeavoured to give him the impression that a relative of mine had invented them. After all, I had a great-grandfather and an uncle who were sea-going. He gave me the boat and shoved off.

When I reckoned that my dead reckoning was dead right I shipped the oars and hoisted the sail, managing, by some accident, to get it right way up. There was very little wind and our motion through the water was practically imperceptible, but I was content enough to recline on the after thwart (which is known in buses as the back seat) humming a verse or two of 'Shenandoah'.

In that vanished era, around nine in the morning, a large number of Clyde steamers foregathered at Gourock pier. Until that morning I had not appreciated just how many did so. The *Davaar* or the *Dalriada* would be setting out for Campbeltown, via Lochranza, while the *Duchess of Hamilton* would be getting up steam for the Kyles and Arran. The skipper of the *Columba* would be looking up the almanac for conditions at Tarbert, while the mate of the *King Edward* would be wiping the remains of his haddie and egg from his chin before asking the chief engineer if he had enough coal on the fire to make the Kilbrannan Sound. Less important vessels would be getting ready to sail for less foreign parts, like Dunoon, Rothesay and Carrick Castle.

I have learned since, and on good authority, for I know many
of the Clyde skippers, that these boats had been doing this for years
and years without ever getting in one another's way. But there
has to be a first time for everything, and this was it. Wafted along
by a light air was the lugsail, with myself at the tiller, half-way
through the second verse of 'Blow the Man Down'. I was thinking
that the melody went rather well to the accompaniment of a number
of ships' hooters, set pleasantly in different keys. It was like singing
an aria from an oratorio to the accompaniment of a great organ.
I felt that it was quite moving.

It then occurred to me that possibly someone was trying to attract
my attention. Somebody was: about fifteen ships' officers. Occasionally I awake in the middle of the night and see these ships. Every
time I do I seem to see more of them.

I appreciated for the first time exactly how Sir Richard Grenville
felt when, after leaving Flores in the Azores, he found himself in
the middle of the Spanish fleet.

Some of these Clyde steamers were going forward, some backward,
while some were doing the apparently impossible and going side-
ways. They were of all shapes and sizes and colour of funnel, but
all had one thing in common. Leaning over the bridge of each
steamer was a gentleman wearing a cap with a white top, and with
a red face. With one hand each clasped the piece of string which
operates the hooter, while the other was brandished in my direction
in what at first I thought to be a friendly salutation, but which I
realized almost immediately to be a threatening gesture. They were
all shouting at once, and this confused me.

Had they appointed someone to speak for all, all might have been
well. But I suppose the last thing to expect from a convocation of
ships' captains, all of highland origin, and all from different islands,
is unanimity. I gathered that they wished me to lower the sail.
Which I did, forgetting that I was standing immediately underneath
it. The sound of swearing grew more muffled, but did not really
reduce in volume or in pungency.

They used words like port and starboard. From what I had seen
of them I would not assume that they were judges of starboard, but
they all looked as if they might be fair judges of port. They exhausted the English language, dredging it to its very depths, and

C

then reverted to their native Gaelic. I have been told that the Gaelic is the great language for the love-making, having no fewer than nineteen words for 'darling'. I doubt if any of them was used that day.

The fact that I am writing these words some fifty years later is proof enough that I survived. I do not know how, and I suppose that any of these captains, now still alive, will wonder why.

I rowed ashore and met the boat hirer who had been having fits on the beach for the last half-hour. I handed him my shilling and waited for the change, which was not forthcoming. I decided not to press the matter, lest worse befall. Since then I have not indulged myself in yachting.

In 1923 in Glasgow the BBC opened 5 SC, Scotland's broadcasting station, which made its first broadcast on my fifteenth birthday. This was not mentioned in the celebration of the BBC's jubilee. I hope it was merely an oversight.

In school I was doing reasonably well, and had been promised my first new bicycle if I passed my Intermediate in all seven subjects. In those days seven subjects meant rather more than seven subjects means today. English included history and geography. Maths included algebra, geometry and arithmetic, and science included everything which by a stretch of the imagination could be called a science subject. The others were French, Latin, art (which we called drawing) and another one whose name I have forgotten. I learned early that I was destined neither to be a mathematician nor a scientist.

Sanny Dunlop, one of the maths masters, would say: 'Dow, you can get the wrong answer quicker than anybody else in the class,' and so I could.

Algebra I could just manage; geometry I did not really mind, but arithmetic was my despair. I think too much. When faced with an arithmetical problem involving poles and chains and things, or bills of parcel sums which could be dealt with far better by the chap on the other side of the counter, I would begin to dream. All sorts of lovely thoughts would flood into my mind. And this is not the way to do sums. You know the kind of sum?

'If it takes five men three days to dig a field of five acres, three roods and six poles, how long will it take 1043 men to dig a field half the size?'

This kind of sum seemed plain silly to me, and still does. It does not cover all the facts and take into account all the contingencies. There is no allowance for leaning on shovels, or spitting on the hands and eating their piece, and blowing their noses with the thumb applied to the side of the nostril in the fascinating way navvies have, and which my doctor long ago assured me is the best way to blow the nose without doing damage to the organ.

So, faced with such a sum, I would go into a trance and think up other problems such as: 'If it takes a man a week to walk a fortnight, how many yards of black pudding will it take to make a bracelet for a left-handed canary?'

I never put this particular problem to Sanny Dunlop, for reasons that will be plain to anyone who knew Sanny.

Had there been a prize for English in each class, I think I would have won it. Unfortunately there was not. I did get a prize for Latin, however, and this was to be my last.

The gold medal in the Secondary was for English and I had my heart set on it, but I was cheated. They decided to award the gold medal to the *dux* of the school in all subjects. This removed it far from my reach. I have since forgiven them for doing this, but I did not at the time.

I loved English. I loved learning the screeds and screeds of poetry which we had to learn. Big hunks of Shakespeare and Gray, and Shelley and Keats and Chaucer. This, to me, was no labour at all. And I loved to write essays, which were called 'Composition'. The trouble was that when my fingers tried to keep pace with my mind, the handwriting got worse and worse till they decided I had better do it all over again.

The weekend composition was supposed to consist of two pages of a foolscap essay book without lines. Careful authors, by spacing out the lines generously, and having plenty of paragraphs, and beginning and ending each line as far as possible away from the edge of the page, could manage their statutory coverage in a matter of minutes. Not so Dow! As long as there was paper available, I was there to fill it.

After one effort, the English teacher, called Thomson and a sar-

castic type as so many good teachers are, appended his comment.
It read (I subsequently ascertained): 'Rewrite. I do not propose
to purchase a microscope with which to decipher your calligraphy.'
The trouble was that I couldn't make out his writing and took the
book out of his desk and asked him to explain. I got belted for
giving up cheek.

But the epic achievement in essay writing was in Johnny Bell's
class. Johnny was a very thorough teacher, if a little lacking in imagination. The subject was the Siege of Troy, and I fairly let myself go.
I had Menelaus bursting through the ruins to where white Helen
sat. Though, even knowing my Rupert Brooke, I made no reference
to 'that adulterous whore'. I doubt if I knew what an adulterous
whore was, anyway. I had Hector dragged round the walls, and
Achilles sulking in his tent with his sore tendon, an affliction for
which I had to have an operation through trying to shove a car up a
hill in Greenock. I had Laocoon, and the serpents, and the wooden
horse and everything. I covered pages and pages.

Johnny Bell rejected that essay seven times. This is no exaggeration. Seven times he rejected it and made me rewrite it. I had to
stay in after school and do it. Each time I tried just to copy what
I had already written in better penmanship. But each time the thing
ran away with me again.

This was a joke of dear old Johnny's for years afterwards: 'The
Siege of Troy in seven parts by J. L. Dow.' I didn't grudge Johnny
his joke. He had very few to start with.

There were two other English teachers who had some influence on
me. One was a young teacher called Dewar Robb, whose uncle, of
the same name, was senior history teacher in the Grammar. Dewar
Robb decided that Paisley Grammar should have a school magazine
and he selected me as one of the junior editors. He discovered that
I had some talent for parody. I think it must have been an essay I
wrote for another English teacher, Miss Anderson. It had something
to do with Doctor Johnson. I tried to write it as Boswell would have
written it. The thing appealed to Miss Anderson and she must have
shown it to Dewar Robb. He presented me with a book of parodies.
I loved them. There was one about Hiawatha's camera. But
anybody can parody Hiawatha. I strove for more challenging
things.

We still got this weekend essay. We did an immense amount of homework, and it did us no harm. In fact it did us a great deal of good, and the modern child would be the better for more of it. Though I think that one of the reasons why teachers don't hand out so much homework is that they will not trust mothers and fathers with the responsibility of helping in the education of their children. Like the headmaster who said that the only people who should not be allowed to have children were parents.

I wrote essays for Miss Anderson, and she was a very good teacher indeed. In fact I think she became in later life chairman of the Educational Institute of Scotland. Which, of course, doesn't prove that she was a very good teacher, though, indeed, she was. Now and then she would read bits of my essays in class, to indicate to the others what they might do if they became ambitious. But I remember that several times she would write in her critique of my literary effort: 'Try to avoid this tendency to sermonize at the end of your essay.'

I did not take her advice then. I have not been taking it since. But this, too, I have observed. If you are going to moralize at the end of an essay, you must have an essay first. You must have a carefully prepared, well-written, punctuated and polished work of literature to present to intelligent people, before you can draw any moralistic conclusions. Too many men in the ministry forget this, or have never known this. But this is true not of the ministry alone.

How many after-dinner speakers have you suffered under, who think that they can just throw out a word or two off the cuff, and be a great success? A good after-dinner speaker can give the impression that he is doing this. But he isn't. He has done his homework. And you'll never be a speaker, a preacher, or a writer, unless you do. Some may call it genius. The geniuses call it sweat.

But this, again, is a digression. Back in the early twenties, Paisley Grammar was the only Secondary school in the town. The John Neilson, and the Camphill went up only to Intermediate level, which meant that the pupils of these schools who had any ambitions in the direction of university had to come to the Grammar to get finished off. This made competition rather keen.

To begin with you had three school *duxes* in confrontation. Deciding that this was not in the true spirit of education, I withdrew from

the competition. Though I was prepared to take on the best of them
at English.

In the Secondary, and for some reason I have not even yet understood, I elected to take Greek. I had, at that time, no thoughts of
the ministry, though Miss Anderson was a wee bit worried about
my moralizing. She may have seen the shadows falling before the
coming events. I did not. I think I was trying to get away from
mathematics.

Only two of us took Greek: Tommy Macdougall and myself.
There are only two reasons for taking Greek in school. One is that
you are going to be a minister and the other is that you are going to
be a teacher of classics. And a teacher of classics is one who wants
to train others either to be ministers or teachers of classics who will
train others to be either ministers or teachers of classics.

Of course, this is all changed nowadays. My old friend and fellow
class-mate, Professor Willie Barclay (he was at one end of the class
and I was at the other; though he was only a member of the football
team and I was the captain), tells me that they don't need Greek
now to get into college. They don't need Hebrew either. I got the
Greek all right, but Hebrew baffled me. This will appear later.

What my future was to be I did not know. Possibly the editorship
of *The Times* was beckoning, but I had no shorthand and could
not type. But the idea of becoming a minister must have been
there.

There is a possibility that my reason for taking Greek was that the
maths masters, with tears streaming down their cheeks, had pleaded
with me to abandon maths and science in the secondary. They
must have felt that this would be too much for them. I agreed.
Not that I was thinking about them. I knew that it would be too
much for me. So it was Greek, Latin, French, and English, with
some odd things, like art, thrown in.

There were fewer distractions in school than there are nowadays,
if distraction is the word for drama clubs and operatic clubs and
debating societies and philatelic organizations. We had none of these.
Nor was there all this business of being presented for your Highers
or not presented for your Highers.

If the Rector thought you hadn't much of a chance, he told
your parents; but if they decided that you should have a bash, you

got the chance to have a bash. And if it came off, the Rector was as delighted as he was surprised.

One possible fault in the system was that you could finish too young. I did. I finished in 1925, and went up to Glasgow University when, physically and mentally, I was still a schoolboy.

In the meantime rugby football had come to Paisley Grammar, by decision of the teachers. This was resented by those who had made the soccer team, which I hadn't. I approved, for I made the rugby team. The soccer addicts had been allowed to continue till their schooldays were over, which made competition for a place in the fifteen rather less fierce.

13. I Can Cook Too

I have mentioned that Mother and Uncle Fred had been left orphans in Dundee at a very early age. Mother went into domestic service, and I wish I could remember some stories she told about a whaler family she worked for in Tayport. We don't pay enough attention to these stories at the time.

Uncle Fred went to sea at the age of around twelve, and came home from his first voyage when he was fourteen and a half. There used to be a picture in our house of the full-rigged ship *Dundee* of Captain Jarvis. There were photographs of all the members of the crew, including Uncle Fred, who was an apprentice or a third mate. I wish I knew where that picture got lost when the old home was broken up; for then I would find it again and give it honoured place. For I was very fond of Uncle Fred, though I had never known him in the days of his strength.

He was doing very well at sea, and had a bright future, with, I think, Paddy Henderson's but he met with an accident, and when he was taken off ship gangrene had set in to his leg. He was brought to Mavisbank when I was a very small boy. I have no recollection of it, but Father told me years later. He was very fond of Uncle Fred too, and, I think, rather envied him, because Uncle Fred had been and had seen.

Uncle Fred was in bed, and it was left to Father to tell him that his leg would have to be amputated. Uncle Fred just leaned across the bed and picked up his pipe from the table, lit it, and watched his future go up in smoke.

They offered him a teaching job in a navigation school, but he was a bachelor and undemanding. He took over the weighbridge under the Victoria Arch on Dundee docks, and found much pleasure in entertaining other ancient mariners, who would tell one another tales of what never was on land or sea.

Both Uncle Fred and Father were very keen supporters of Dundee Football Club, Father having played at one time for a team called, I think, Dundee Violet. The first match I ever saw was between Dundee and Third Lanark one Christmas Day, when I must have been a very small boy indeed.

One year Uncle Fred made pilgrimage from Dundee to see a Cup final between his team and Clyde. This would be 1910 or 1911. I heard about this years later.

Clyde were two goals up with minutes to go, and Father suggested to Uncle Fred that it would be as well to depart before the crowd came out, Uncle Fred having an artificial leg to lug around. They hadn't even reached the tram-car before Dundee had equalized. Reading about it in the papers was little consolation for a man who had come all that way with a wooden leg, or for Father, who had left early in sympathy.

Round about Christmas each year, or it may have been New Year, Grandfather and Uncle Fred would come to stay with us, bearing gifts. Later, when we were a bit older, Uncle Fred would anticipate the festive season by sending each of us a new ten-shilling note. Which was quite a sum.

Elsie and I always bought our Christmas presents together, but this could not be done till Uncle Fred's donation arrived. We then sallied forth. For Mother there was a bottle of Californian Poppy perfume. Why we chose this I do not know. Maybe it was the smell that appealed to us; maybe the shape of the bottle. Maybe it wasn't so dear as some of the others. Father got a box of Marcella cigars. I may add that the box contained only five cigars.

Mother, having been in service, was very particular about our manners, at table and away from table. We did not dine out except when we went to the pantomime at Christmas. And this is something which parents do not pay enough attention to. I may be old-fashioned, but there's a way to hold a knife and fork, and a way to break a dinner roll, and a way to put marmalade on your toast. And these are the right ways: these are the ways tested by time. They are not just conventions. The right way is always the natural way. But don't let me go on with this.

I remember once coming in late for tea. I must have had some good reason, otherwise I would not have got any tea. The table had been cleared, and Mother asked me what I would like. I said that I fancied scrambled eggs and would make them myself. Actually it was not in the plural, but in the singular.

It turned out very singular indeed, did that egg. Mother had asked me if I knew how to make scrambled egg. I said, almost indignantly, that I would never have dreamed of suggesting I would make the dish if I had not known. She told me not to make a mess, and went on with darning stockings, which was more or less a full-time job.

After some little time in the scullery I came into the kitchen with the pan and suggested that there must have been something wrong with that egg. She asked if I was in the habit of making scrambled egg with boiling water. I tried to give the impression that I had done this in the interests of economy.

She told me that there are two schools of thought on the making of scrambled egg, some cooks using a little milk, others nothing but egg and butter. She then asked what I proposed to do with the mess.

I said it was in my mind to deposit it in the pail which stood below the sink for the accommodation of waste. She said I would do no such thing. Having neglected to ask advice I could eat the end product. That egg did me no good, though possibly the lesson did. Since then scrambled egg has been my favourite kind of egg. I am rather good at it.

From an early age I have been interested in cooking, which, after all, played a large part in Boy Scout training. Lex and I both joined the 25th Renfrewshire at the age of eleven, which gave him a headstart over me. By the time I was of age, he was a patrol leader.

No cooking expertise was needed to qualify for the Tenderfoot badge, but it was necessary for the Second Class badge, the stipulated menu being tea, sausages and potatoes, cooked of course over an open fire in a billy can, which was about the most unsuitable implement ever invented. Some boys, coming for their test, would bring sliced sausages, but to the purist these are not true sausages, and could not possible have been in Baden-Powell's mind when he instituted the badge.

Our scoutmaster advised us to prick the sausages with a fork. Possibly he thought they might otherwise explode This is, of course, as unnecessary as it is undesirable, but we did what we were told.

The child is father of the man, as I have said before. The first time I cooked for a Burns Supper I pricked the haggises as I had been taught as a little lad to prick the sausages, and was left with something that looked like a potful of hot caviare with seven burst balloons floating in it

A few years later St James' Church started a Scout troop and we were transferred to it. Because of my wide experience I was made leader of the Peewit patrol. The colours were green and white but we did not mind, not being connected with the Orange Order. My interest in cooking grew, but did not come to its full flower until during my assistantship and charges in Glasgow and Greenock, I became involved with the Boys' Brigade.

The difference between Scout camps and BB camps is that the BB get their food spoiled for them, while the Scouts spoil their own. I always took on the office of cook, and cooking for thirty or forty boys takes quite a bit of doing.

Boys are very conservative. They won't eat anything they don't get at home. They will view macaroni and cheese with suspicion, yet it is a most useful meal at camp, being both cheap and filling. You could persuade them to have a go by telling them that if they didn't they would get nothing else. Then, later, a boy who had taken his first forkful expecting to be poisoned, would come up some days later and ask when we were going to have thon Spanish stuff with the cheese again.

In Greenock we used to deal with a firm of canteen caterers who had very good lines of tinned goods. One year we were trying to raise money for a pipe band and I wrote to this firm and offered to give them daily menus for a camp of forty if they would give me twenty-five pounds for the band. They thought it was a good idea. They could send this recipe book to distracted BB captains all over the country. I did the job. They sent it back.

Their dietician (a woman) reported that this was not a balanced diet. Imagine putting a Boys' Brigade camp on a balanced diet when they have been stuffing themselves with ice cream and crisps all morning, and chew bubble gum between courses.

14. Pen and Pulpit

In an earlier chapter I mentioned an affection for Jeffery Farnol and a passion for his heroines. Because of this it was from Jeffery Farnol that I earned my first half-guinea in journalism.

A firm of stationers in Paisley started a fiction library when this was a bit of a novelty, and they invited anyone to write an appreciation of any novelist whose works appeared upon their shelves. I wrote an appreciation of Jeffery Farnol and collected my ten and six. It was to be many a long day before I collected another, though I will say I kept on trying.

By the time I was eighteen I could have papered the walls of my attic bedroom with rejection slips. *Chambers's Journal* had a particularly polite rejection slip which insisted that it was only pressure on space which moved them to send my contribution back. It was such a polite rejection slip that I once examined it carefully to ascertain if there were some traces of editorial tears. I have learned since, and by hard experience, that editors do not weep.

Paisley, of course, was a very literary town. If Dundee produced jute, jam and journalists, Paisley produced poets and pirns, and since I was a product of both towns the break-through had to come eventually. I had not realized how long 'eventually' can be.

Like many provincial papers the *Paisley Daily Express* was always happy to publish contributions to its Poets' Corner. Father was a fairly regular contributor. I still have some of his efforts: one on the Irish troubles of the day, which finished with the lines:

> So Patrick dear just rest content,
> And keep this in your view;
> That when Conservatives fall out
> The Liberals get their due.

There was another which he wrote, I would think, when Dr

Fraser was organizing the Forward Movement in the United Free Church. It was called *Kirk Repairs*.

Sir: the kirks am I tae understand are seeking frae their members,
Sic help as ane and a' can gie, tae raise up frae the embers
O' things hurt sair by lowe o' war, a renovated building
Wi' wider doors and brighter lights and gowd instead o' gilding?
They dinna say just 'Reconstruct'; sic things are for the nation;
Yet I wad fain hae them begin again frae the foundation:
Our Lord and Saviour Jesus Christ, and build tae a new planning
On lines sae different that there'd be no' muckle auld left standing.
For lang I, right or wrang, hae thought the pulpit's main concernment
Was that their flock should dodge the deil, though all around should
       ferment.
Tae rest content, if each could dae the things that were expeckit,
Frae worthy members o' their kirks, and leave the rest negleckit.
They aye were quick tae grow white het o'er things ecclesiastic,
But when the nation sought reforms, they'd steer far north o' drastic.
Just look alang the bygane years at social legislation,
At schemes o' welfare for the folk, and uplift tae the nation;
And seek tae find what share the kirk can tae itsel' tak' credit,
Ye'll find, thought Christ inspired the work, 'twas no' His kirk that
       led it.
When revolution, riot, war loomed big, men found it sleeping
And used sic tools tae force a door whase key the kirk was keeping.
Nae wonder then, when social wrangs men seek tae hae correckit,
They gang for help on ither roads whaur help can be expeckit.
When every social question raised demands a moral solving,
Why should the kirk let ithers lead the way tae it's evolving?
Sir, it maun lead, and no' be led: become the world's pleader,
And aye put in a word for Christ when men seek for a leader.
It mauna plead, while slaves exist, that ither men in patience
Should drudge their days, yet glorify their God in sic-like stations.
It mauna rest while at its door conditions eat like cancer
The soul and body o' the folk, but ca' the powers tae answer.
That sic-like things nae mair persist tae sink their roots the deeper;
But boldly lead reforms that mak' ilk man his brither's keeper.
There's nae need that it should tak' sides, turn Liberal or Tory;
Just let it build on the sure plan: that man's good is God's glory.

When John White launched his Church Extension campaign I was a young minister in Glasgow. I resurrected these lines, gave them a twist towards Church Extension, sent them to the old *Glasgow Evening News,* and got twelve and six for it then.

But this was good thinking, and there were many thinking along similar lines. It's a pity the church hadn't listened to them, for a church cannot call itself a reformed church unless, under God, it is constantly reforming itself. So I learned, early on, that the only critic who is worth paying any attention to is the loyal critic who is trying to change things from inside. Not the one who is standing outside throwing stones.

These were ideas that were in our home when I was young, and these ideas stick. They were not preached at us. They were just part of the atmosphere and they were breathed and absorbed. Social justice, Liberalism, and the church in the van of progress. The roots of that planting went very deep, and from them two ministers grew.

This may be the appropriate time to say something about the church, though in time it's jumping ahead of events a little. I went up to college in 1929. (Actually I went up in 1928, but a slight disagreement between me and the examiners in Hebrew lost me a year – for three marks.)

The year 1929 was the union year between the Old Kirk, the Church of Scotland, and the United Free Church, of which we were members. So that, along with a sadly decreasing number, I am a member of the first Trinity Year Club.

After all these years I still have my doubts about the wisdom of that union, which really hasn't taken place yet, for it has resulted in the closure of a great many 'redundant' churches, and each closure has inspired controversy which the church could have been doing without. It has given Presbyteries a bad name, for Presbyterians are great respecters of Presbyteries until they and the Presbytery fail to see eye to eye. Then they are Congregationalists.

But, among other things, the union involved a political compromise, and though there is a time and place for compromise, it usually involves a surrender, or at least a modification, of principle on one side or the other; and sometimes on both sides.

By 1929 the difference between the Parish Church and the Free and United Presbyterian Churches had largely disappeared. But there were differences of mood and of outlook. In the main (though there were exceptions) the UF's were teetotal and Liberal. The Old Kirk took a dram and were Tory. Because of the unfermented wine generally used at the UF communion service, they were known as the 'Jeelie-water kirk'. At the sacrament in the Old Kirk there was a bouquet of vintage port.

The United Church, after 1929, had to make a political compromise, and from that day on, have hardly criticized a government for anything, and I think it is rather significant, though it is maybe mere coincidence, that in the year in which the change took place in the Church, the Labour Party came to power in the Commons.

St James' Church, as I have mentioned before, was a middle-class and well-off church, blessed with a succession of excellent preachers, since, among other advantages, St James' could afford to pay them. From one of them, especially, I learned a great deal: he was Alastair Stewart. As a student, we were led to understand, he had played for Heart of Midlothian, and that was enough to commend him to me, even if he had been deaf and dumb, which he assuredly was not.

He was a master of the English language: something, you will have gathered, that I appreciated. There was never anything shoddy about his work. I have tried to follow his example. And when there were times when pressure of work kept me from giving my sermons all the attention they should have been given, and I went into the pulpit with something not properly thought out and put together, and somebody came to me after service and said that was a grand sermon, I have felt ashamed.

In the normal way, I will not pretend that I have not delivered myself of some tripe on occasion, but I take pride in the fact that it has usually been well-prepared tripe. And well-prepared tripe is, at least, digestible. It can also be nourishing.

Alastair Stewart was a bachelor, and his children's addresses suffered somewhat in consequence. But in those days most children's addresses tended to be a wee bit dull. A smile was permissible in church, but laughter was rather frowned upon. The minister would always insist on having a text: that magical peg on which to hang a few thoughts. As if all the words of wisdom that were ever spoken were contained between the boards of the Bible.

Children's addresses, and quite a number of sermons, can do

fine without a text. Something for the kids to look at is much better. One wee chap told me that he always liked to see an object in the pulpit. I looked at him for a long minute to make sure he was not making anything personal out of it. But I took his word for it. Any time I do not have an object in the pulpit for a children's address, I apologize to them. And, of course, this goes for a lot of sermons too.

There was one minister who selected as his text 'God tempers the wind to the shorn lamb', and wrote a powerful oration on the theme. On the Sunday morning he looked up Cruden's *Concordance* to find chapter and verse for the authority for his discourse, and discovered to his amazement that the words are not in Holy Writ at all.

Most lambs on this island, if they are born when the wind is tempered, are born when the wind is bad-tempered. They don't shear them either. But I will say that in this village, with so many sheep on the road and all looking for a way into the gardens, any organist who played for a voluntary *Sheep may safely graze* would be in danger of getting lynched on the Monday. Nobody would think of doing it on the Sunday.

Another minister who greatly impressed me was Andrew Kennedy of Lamlash, whom we sat under when we were on holiday. These men were craftsmen at their job, and they were well aware that their job was communication. There's no point in having ideas unless you can communicate them.

I always love to see or hear a craftsman at work; and it doesn't matter in the slightest what the work is. It can be sculpture, painting, writing, preaching, ironing a shirt or laying bricks. Craftsmanship must come out. And craftsmanship can't come out unless it is put in. Nobody becomes a craftsman at anything without work. There can be an element of genius to begin with, but there's a lot of geniuses who aren't craftsmen, and, by the same token, a lot of craftsmen who aren't geniuses.

Far be it from me to criticize the training for the ministry, who am one who did not take full advantage of it when it was offered, and who does not know what it amounts to today. But the main job of those who teach divinity students is to make them craftsmen at their job, and the job is the preaching of the Word, before all else.

They've shoved the pulpit over to the side now, and given pride of place to the communion table. Fair enough; it doesn't matter where the pulpit is so long as there's a man in it who has something to say and knows how to say it, and who has thought hard enough, and worked hard enough, and prayed hard enough, before he goes into the pulpit, so that he feels entitled to preface his sermon with the thought: 'Thus saith the Lord'. Which is the prophetic way.

There was once a very devout and completely incompetent village joiner; and there was a very competent but rather agnostic village cobbler.

'Aye, Sandy,' said the joiner one day, trying to conclude an interminable argument on theology. 'But you canna mak' a star.'

'Man, Erchie,' said the cobbler, turning back to his last, 'and you canna mak' a barra.'

With which profound remark I close this chapter.

15. Joyful Sounds

Among my many regrets is that I was never 'sent to music'. For I am very fond of music. We did not have a piano. We had an American organ on which Father could play tunes in the key of C, apparently unaware that there were any others. And for some inexplicable reason he seemed to have the idea that there is some difference between the music for an organ and the music for a piano. For this, or for some other reason, probably because I did not express any particular desire to learn, I was not 'sent to music'.

I didn't miss it at the time, though I'm sorry now. This happens with more important matters than music. However I learned to play that organ off the sol-fah notation which was drummed into us at school by Daddy Reid, and to play not just in the key of C. When I showed this manuscript to sister Elsie she asked me if I remembered going down on my hands and knees to work the pedals by hand so that she could play to my blowing, her legs not being long enough to reach down.

Although those who know me, or who may have heard me broadcasting, may not believe it, I was, as a boy, a fairly good treble singer. I could long for the wings of a dove with the best of them, though it would take a fairly well-developed tree to hold a nest in the wilderness for me nowadays.

My ambition was to get into the church choir, though they did not accept trebles, having plenty of competent sopranos. This may seem an odd ambition to those who do their best to keep out of a church choir, but if you got into St James' choir under Dr Rigby you had accomplished something.

The whole congregation of St James' stood for the anthem, and if they did not have anthem books with music, there were in the pews books with the words, so that at least they knew what the anthem was all about.

It's an odd thing, you know, that the pop singer is the one who gives clear enunciation to words that aren't worth hearing, while the classy singer, with words that are worth hearing, is usually incomprehensible.

I shared an anthem book with Father, who had a fairish baritone voice, and in the same pew were Andrew Lang and his wife, both ex-choristers, Andrew being a tenor. At the other end of the pew were two school-teachers, the Misses Russell, who sang contralto. We were quite a wee choir on our own in pew twenty-four.

Mrs Lang was an elderly body and a dear soul. She wore a fur coat on Sundays, and when I was wee she would put her arm round me when sermon time came and I would sleep away in an odour of sanctity whose principal ingredient was mothballs. Even today, in the unlikely event of my being unable to get to sleep, they would not have to prescribe phenobarbitone. If they held a mothball under my nose I would drop off in a matter of seconds and become a little boy again with my face in a sealskin coat.

But it was the big choir I had set my heart on; so when my voice broke I proferred my services. I was surprised that a certificate of character was not required. This was probably because our family was known to be respectable. There was, however, a severe and searching test of voice, and of ability to read.

For one reason or another Dr Rigby decided that if I was to get into the choir at all it would not be on the tenor side. So I took my place among the basses (at practice only, I hasten to add). You had to serve a probationary period before you made the choir and became one of the elect.

You turned up for every practice. If you didn't, you were out on your ear; and every Sunday, hoping that one of the basses would be down with cholera, you would turn out hoping to get his place. If there was a vacancy you got in. If there wasn't you went back to the family pew and sang your heart out in the hope that Dr Rigby would hear you above the rest, and be full of remorse.

St James' Church was very keen on foreign missions, and had a Missionary Society. They held an annual general meeting, and it was almost traditional that the youngest member of the choir (I had made it by this time – one of the basses must have died or been pensioned off) was invited to be soloist. I explained that I had no songs.

This was not quite true. I could have sung something we got in school, but not the melody line, and the bass part tends to be rather dull when taken alone. I could have sung a verse or two of 'She was poor but she was honest', and of similar ballads with which we entertained one another and were never any the worse for it. I could have reduced them to tears with 'Your baby has gone down the plug-hole' which I taught years later to our grandchildren. But I felt that these were not appropriate to the occasion.

The secretary of the Society said she would look out something of her father's, and bass songs never die, or even date. We basses do not get the kind of song with which you could entertain or serenade a *señorita*, accompanied by a guitar.

Bass songs always have something to do with the sea, and battles, and deeds of derring-do, and drink, and cavalry charges, and drink, and lost causes, and more drink. She produced one of each kind. The first was a pathetic ballad of the sea entitled 'I shall come home when the ebb-tide flows'. The other was 'I am a friar of orders grey'. I thanked her and took them home to practise.

'I shall come home' is a sad song. The composer meant it to be a sad song. But never, even in his more depressed moments, could he possibly have imagined that it was as sad as it sounded when an uncertain bass, aged seventeen, was trying to transcribe the staff notation into sol-fa on an American organ.

In the fullness of time came the night of the annual meeting of the Missionary Society, and I turned up, torn between a desire not to return home till the ebb-tide flowed, and an offer to serve the Society by going out to Manchuria. I had not rehearsed the songs with an accompanist. The accompanist started the introduction.

This was the first time I had heard it. I thought it rather nice. I thought that she was maybe just trying out the piano, or getting the stiffness out of her fingers. She stopped.

I learned subsequently that this was the place where I was supposed to come in. When nothing happened she looked up and smiled pleasantly. Being well brought up, I returned her smile, and she started all over again. Once more we exchanged courtesies,

though I thought her smile a trifle strained this time. I was beginning
to feel that we were letting the audience down, and that this might
have an adverse effect on the collection for foreign missions which
would be taken subsequently. After all, they had not come out on
a wet night to hear a woman, however talented, play variations on
a theme from 'I shall come home when the ebb-tide flows'. They had
come to hear Dow sing. She must have thought the same, for she
whispered: 'Will I give you your note, Jimmy?'

I refrained from mentioning that this was precisely what I had
been waiting for for the last two minutes. I merely indicated that
if it was all right with her it was all right with me. And between us
we got the ebb-tide flowing. And in response to an enthusiastic
reception, which was probably caused by relief that I had managed
to get started at all, I favoured the company with 'I am a friar of
orders grey'. This launched me on an unprofitable career as a
vocalist.

Our minister by this time was Lewis Sutherland, himself a fine
bass singer, and whose wife was an even finer soprano singer. After
the Missionary Society meeting she told Father and Mother that
she thought my voice had possibilities. They did not say that for me
they had ambitions not connected with the open-air sale of coal.
She said that with practice and application I might yet be a singer.
I had thought I was a singer already, but it seemed that I was wrong.
So twice a week after school I went to the manse and practised
scales. Great big long strings of notes which you sang to *ah*, and
oo, and *eeh*. It would have wrung the vowels of mercy.

We proceeded from there to the bass solos from *The Messiah*.
This went on for some time till I went up to university and had no
more time for such frivolities. I fell back on Angus, who lived in
the next close and was teaching himself staff notation, also on an
American organ. We collaborated. I was the vocalist, Angus the
accompanist.

What it did for his playing, I do not know, but it fairly helped
my breathing. I had to spend minutes hanging on to a note which
Angus had found for me till he got the next one sorted out, and his
fingers properly arranged for the next chord. It was easy enough
for the organ to find the wind as long as Angus kept pedalling. For
me it was murder, but it developed the chest.

We reached the heights in a song called 'Anchored', which told more or less the same story as 'I shall come home'. No sailor who leaves port in a bass song ever comes home alive. This song was true to form. The ship went down with all hands, and she was left sitting on the pier.

But mony a cantie day Angus and I had at the organ, and, like Nannie in *Tam o' Shanter*, 'Perished mony a bonnie boat'.

16. Exams and Excursions

Although my teachers spent many sleepless nights trying to discover what kind of mind I had, they came to only one conclusion. This was on the kind of mind I did not have – namely a mind receptive to mathematics, or to what, in those days, was loosely referred to as 'science'.

This included physics, chemistry, botany, and various 'ics' and 'ologies'. But not, if I remember aright, biology. They assumed either that we were too young for that, or that we already knew as much about us as was good for us.

To pass your Intermediate in maths you had to satisfy the examiners in arithmetic, algebra and geometry, which were treated as one subject. So were English, history and geography: all the one subject, and on your knowledge of all three you passed or failed.

I got the lot, along with French, Latin, art (which we called drawing), Greek, and there must have been something else: possibly woodwork or gymnastics. There were seven altogether; and as a reward I got my first bicycle. I knew how to ride a bicycle, of course. Indeed I had learned to ride a bicycle in the village of Alloway, years before. It was a lady's bicycle, of a brown colour, and the first time I was on it the thing got away from me, and I hit Burns' cottage full on. Many years later I forgave Robert for being born in such a hard cottage, and have given many speeches in his immortal memory.

But anyway the teachers decided, either separately or in conference assembled, that for my sake, to say nothing of the advancement of their own careers, I should drop mathematics and science, and devote myself to the study of the classics.

Archimedes thereupon went back to his bath, and Diogenes emerged from his tub.

My main complaint with mathematics was that I, a mere schoolboy, should be required to prove all over again what had been proved two thousand years ago, and accepted by all succeeding generations.

There was, for example, this chap Pythagoras, who had discovered, either by accident or design, that in a right-angled triangle the square on the hypotenuse is equal to the sum of the squares on the other two sides. Although I had never met Pythagoras personally, and so had no opportunity to assess his character, I was perfectly prepared, on the evidence, to accept that he was an honourable man who would never have dreamed of deceiving a twentieth-century schoolboy on a matter of such importance. My attitude was that if Pythagoras had said so, this was good enough for me. Apart from that, generations of schoolboys had given blood, toil, sweat and tears to verify his statement. It seemed to me that my poor contribution to the sum total of knowledge was superfluous.

Especially since, if my conclusions had been accepted, it would have been proved, beyond all peradventure, that Pythagoras was wrong, and that every roof, built by his formula, was squint.

The abandonment of science, however, had its repercussions later. I went up to university with my mind made up to take an Honours degree in English. I had some vague idea that all that was required was an ability to write essays on any subject under the sun. I discovered that this was not so. I failed in English at my first sitting.

McNeile Dixon was professor of English, and he had published an anthology of English verse entitled *The English Parnassus*. Naturally this was a prescribed book for reading, and the first question on the examination paper was to spot twelve quotations, say where they came from and who wrote them, and try to give the line before and the line after.

I learned later that if you did not get enough of your twelve spots the examiners went no farther and never even got the length of your essay. And I had thought that mine was brilliant. I think it had something to do with Macbeth, my favourite Shakespearian character. I'm still sorry that no one has ever asked me to play the part.

I spent the summer swatting *The English Parnassus*, and passed in September. But by this time I had decided to be a minister, and I asked myself what was the difference between having an Honours degree in English, which I might have made at the second level, but certainly not at the top level, and having an ordinary degree which would still enable me to hang a purple hood down my back when I went into the pulpit. Little did I know what I was in for.

What the requirements are today I do not know. But in Glasgow in the twenties in order to obtain an Ordinary degree as Master of Arts (and I am master of none of them) you had to have English at Ordinary and Higher level (which meant Anglo-Saxon under Ritchie Girvan). You had to have a language other than English: I managed to get through in Latin. You had to have a philosophy: I made moral philosophy. Apart from that, you had to make up a total of seven subjects, and one of them had to be a science subject.

They get away with murder nowadays. Never having had science or maths in my Highers (I would never have passed in them anyway) these were closed to me. What remained? There was geography, and there was geology. I thought that geology was the subject for me, having been on the rocks for many years.

Well, maybe that is wrong. Father had done his bit in keeping us going, but at this point of my university career (if it could be called a career) he had died. I'll come back to this later on.

It was a case of chuck the whole thing, or get on and get finished. I elected to take the shorter course, and get out as soon as possible. But I still had to pass in geology. I wasn't so bad on the Carboniferous, and I wrote some powerful stuff on the Pleistocene, though I always kept getting it mixed with the Plasticine. But when it came to drawing a cross-section of Merthyr Tydfil my mind reeled. In the attempt to understand crystallography it collapsed.

In the end I left university without a degree, and once a year for three years had another bash at geology (except for one year when I went up on the wrong day), and in the end, either because I got a paper which suited me or in tribute to my perseverance they awarded a pass. But this is running ahead of things, for in this blow-by-blow account, schooldays are not yet over. The trouble with this kind of reminiscence is not shortage of material; it is to know what to put in and what to leave out. There was this Red Indian, for example.

At least he said he was a Red Indian, and had long hair to prove it. This was for the purpose of his act, only. At other times he rolled it into a bun and put his bonnet on top of it.

The short broad street between Paisley Abbey and the George A. Clark Town Hall, Abbey Close, was Paisley's Speaker's Corner. Anyone who had anything to sell, or anything to say, and a great many who had nothing to say but were determined to say it, gathered there on a Saturday night. They were joined by those who had nothing better to do, and the Mavisbank lads would patronize it now and then.

One of the salesmen was the Red Indian, who, apart from his long hair, gave further claim to the description by having a fair cargo of firewater. He also had a stock whip, and, drunk or sober, he could use it. He used it to attract the crowd. He would knock a match out of your hand or a cigarette out of your mouth. He would supply the match, but the victim had to supply his own cigarette. His purpose in life, however, was not to display his virtuosity with the whip, but to sell small paper packets of a secret powder guaranteed to cure anything from hay fever to a fractured pelvis. The secret had been discovered by an ancestor of his on the plains of Montana or Milwaukee. It was probably Epsom salts.

But I learned a lesson from this chap that has stood me in good stead in a lifetime of preaching sermons and making speeches. You can hold the attention of an audience for just so long – and it isn't nearly as long as you think. Then you have to get out the whip as this Red Indian did when he saw that the attention of his customers was fading and that they were starting to move off to listen to the man who was trying to prove that the world is round.

It was possible to hold this kind of open-air gathering then when there was practically no traffic along side streets, especially on a Saturday. On the main Glasgow road, of course, there were the tram-cars. Paisley had its own cars, double-deckers without a roof. There were notices on the bridges telling you to keep your head down. I suppose they didn't want their bridges damaged.

But the Paisley trams were eventually taken over by Glasgow Corporation, and they tried a bold experiment which might well be copied today. In order to attract custom they lowered the tariff and instituted a maximum fare of twopence.

This concession was introduced on a Sunday, and the lads decided that we should extend our patronage. So, after church and lunch, five of us set out for Paisley Cross with the intention of travelling to Airdrie, some twenty miles away, and the best value possible for twopence. We were determined to secure the open-air part of the tram which stuck out at the front.

When we reached the Cross we found a queue so long that you nearly had to take a tram to get to the end of it. Inspectors in green coats and with red faces were trying to herd the Buddies into line. Tram after tram came tearing down from Glasgow, the conductor leaped out to swing the pole to the other end, while the driver belted through the car with his various implements.

It was the biggest mass movement of a population since the Exodus. Monotonously, even wearily, the Town Hall clock struck the quarters. The river Cart rose and fell with the tide. At last we got our chance. We nipped on at the wrong end before the driver had got through from the other end, and secured the open-air portion at the front, upstairs. Airdrie, we told one another, here we come.

Being still in school I didn't have a hat, but I had lifted Father's snap brim from the hallstand when I was leaving the house. It blew off in Paisley Road West. I had to get that hat.

The others, being loyal souls, accompanied me downstairs, much to the surprise of the conductor who had not expected to ring the bell this side of Airdrie. I got the hat, and we went to the nearest tram stop to await further transport to Airdrie. We hadn't a hope. We decided we had better call it a day and get back to Paisley, so we crossed the road to another stop.

It then was borne in on us that the entire population of Airdrie, with the assistance of Coatbridge, had decided, for some un-accountable reason, to spend the day in Paisley.

I suggested that we should walk down Plantation Street, cross the Clyde by the ferry, and get a tram to Yoker, recrossing by Renfrew Ferry, and so home. I felt that a sail would be good for us. We found that the whole population of Barrhead was on its way to Dalmuir. We walked, and got home eventually, I to be informed that Father had had to wear his bowler hat to evening service and that there would be an inquiry on his return.

The sermon may have been on forgiveness or on righteous judgement, for when I threw myself on the mercy of the court, all he said was that it served me right.

17. A Student of Glasgow

In the last two years of school there was nothing really of any note, and in due season the time for the Highers came and went, and I discovered, somewhat to my surprise, I will admit, and somewhat to the surprise of others, I suspect, that I had passed. Lower Greek had seen me through.

So along with one or two others in Mavisbank it was heigh ho for Gilmorehill. In those days there were no grants. There was a competitive bursary examination for which I did not enter, not wanting to waste the time of the examiners; but obtaining a bursary by examination was more an academic exercise than it was a means to paying the fees. To be a bursar really was something.

The Education Authority distributed a certain amount of money, though parental income had to be pretty low to quality. Father's certainly was not low enough. After the War, when local authority housing began to appear, he was made town planning surveyor for the Upper District of Renfrewshire, most of which has gradually been absorbed into Glasgow. I suppose his salary would be in the neighbourhood of £500 a year, which was not at all bad in the twenties.

We got the Carnegie grant, which was more or less automatic, and just about covered the fees, but Father and Mother had to be responsible for the rest, and there were two of us at university. We got ten shillings a week each, and out of this had to pay our zone ticket to Glasgow, tram fares, such food as we wanted, and the rest was for luxuries. If you wanted to smoke you didn't eat. It was as simple as that. Of course, pie and chips, or egg and chips, cost only coppers, but cigarettes were sixpence for ten, elevenpence ha'penny for twenty, but that was too much to spend all at once.

Lex didn't smoke, and never has. I did. Father knew this before I had left school, of course, as all fathers do, and on the day school was finished he gave me a pipe, a pouch of tobacco and a piece of advice. Which was that if I was determined to smoke I should smoke the pipe. I did for a while and felt quite manly.

It was at this time that I 'joined the church' and decided to go in for the ministry. One of the first I told, after the family, who did not burst into tears and embrace me, was our assistant minister who seemed rather pleased that I, after having seen what it had done for him, had decided to follow on.

It was the practice of the minister after the service of admission to present the new communicants with a card bearing an appropriate text selected by himself. Mine was 'Preach the unsearchable riches of Christ'. In many ways I may not have been as faithful a minister as I might have been, but in obeying the behest of that text I believe that I have. At least I have tried, though at that time I did not realize how unsearchable these riches are.

I am not one who goes in for much in the way of self-analysis, or who asks himself why he elected to become a minister. There was nothing which could be called a 'conversion'. I know people who have been converted. I have seen it happening. There is such an experience, though sometimes, I fear, it is not quite as genuine as the converted imagines it is.

Conversion is like reformation. It is usually regarded as an end, a culmination, but it is nothing of the kind. It is no more than the start of a continuous and continuing process. When the mother asked the wee girl how she had managed to fall out of bed, daughter said: 'I think I went to sleep too near the place where I got in.' The same happens with converts and with churches. Once isn't enough.

I hope I have managed to convey – though the previous pages have been written fairly light-heartedly, as I hope the succeeding pages will be written – something of the 'tone' of our home.

It was a religious home, though we had no family prayers or anything of the sort. A certain standard of behaviour and of attitude was demanded. If in early manhood I had said that I didn't want to go to church, I would not have been made to go to church; though I imagine that Mother would have pleaded with me to go 'to please Father'. It was, within the limits of respectability, a liberal upbringing. But if there was one lesson that was constantly taught it was that any gifts that you had were not for your own enjoyment or for your own profit: that you had them so that you could make a contribution to the total good of humankind.

I think that this was the main reason why I elected to be a minister of the Church of Scotland. Anyway, unlike a great many of today's university students, I went to Glasgow knowing what the end product and purpose was to be.

It is fatally easy to fall to the temptation to compare and contrast; always to your own advantage. But I do think that a great many of the frustrations of students, and even of graduates, today are that they had no particular purpose in becoming students in the first place. I am thankful that I had, though, as will appear, I did not work all that hard to equip myself for my chosen life's work.

There were, as I have said, no university grants, which meant that we, along with a great majority of lads at Glasgow, had neither the money nor the opportunity to enter very deeply into university life. I joined the Liberal Association; the late John Bannerman was president. But my classes were all in the morning, and the Liberal meetings, for debate and the like, were at night. When classes were over I came home for something to eat, and didn't feel inclined to go back. I had no money for any social whirl, and neither had the other chaps in Mavisbank. We had our own way of passing an evening, apart from the necessary study.

With the odd coppers I bought books from the barrows that appeared on every side street off Renfield Street. I still have most of them. They fairly impress visitors, who may, like the villages of Sweet Auburn, wonder that one small head could carry all I knew. Or, at least, all I ought to know with all these books on my shelves. Unfortunately my wife does not encourage visitors to the study. She complains about the mess, though I tell her that a maker of beautiful furniture cannot operate without making shavings. She agrees, but maintains with female logic and insistence that the cabinet-maker sweeps up periodically.

The result of all this was that though I and many others were in university, we were not of it. University, to us, was just a means to an end. Of course we lost something, but I wonder if we lost very much that was important.

For English we had McNeile Dixon, who was a delight on Shake-

speare, and Ritchie Girvan for Anglo-Saxon, which was no delight
to anybody. Phillimore translated Horace and Vatullus into English
which was as beautiful as it was bawdy. In history there were Medley
and Browning: in logic, Bowman, and in moral philosophy, Hetherington.

With one or two stumblings I managed these not too badly. But
there was still geology and Professor Gregory. He was lost on an
expedition up the Amazon, though he looked like a man who could
not have found his way across Sauchiehall Street.

It was in the moral philosophy class that somebody stole my
bowler hat. It was a new hat, which was quite certainly why it was
stolen. It had a splendid red silk lining and it cost seven and six.
Another had been left in its place. If the owner of this other hat
had been charged twopence at a jumble sale he would have been
robbed. It was faintly greenish in hue and was half-full of dandruff.

After class I waited to see Professor Hetherington about my
hat. There was quite a queue waiting to see him; keen types who
wanted further elucidation of the ideas of Plato, Hegel and others.
This took some time, but at length Hetherington turned to me, a
little wearily perhaps, but faithful in his duty to assure the young
feet on the pursuit of moral philosophy.

He asked what he could do for me, and I asked him if he could
get me back my new bowler hat with the red silk lining. He referred
me to the janitor. I was disappointed in Hetherington, though he
later became Vice-Chancellor of, I think, Manchester, and later
returned to the same exalted position in Glasgow.

Next time the class gathered, I felt he had missed a chance. He
should have given a lecture on my bowler hat with the red silk
lining. After all, there was at least one in that class, going to have
a bash at a moral philosophy examination and steeped in the works
of the great from Moses to Emmanuel Kant, who had not a vestige
of morality in him.

I thought that after Hetherington had done justice to that, this
chap would come forward, with tears streaming down his face, and
fall on his knees in front of the rostrum crying: *'Mea culpa! Mea
maxima culpa!'* He would then have handed back the hat.

Hetherington did not accept this challenge. I would have forgiven the chap, of course, as long as I got my hat back. It struck

me later that the chap who had pinched it would probably cut the class for a week or so, in case I recognized it.

The janitor, when I saw him, was most sympathetic. He told me that the moral phil. class had quite a reputation for this kind of thing. He suggested that maybe the fellow had taken it inadvertently and would return it when he discovered his mistake. He did not say this very confidently, however, and when he had seen the hat that had been left he shook his head sorrowfully, and said no more. On my way to the tram I threw the offensive thing into the Kelvin, where, for all I know, it still is.

Before the arts course was finished Father was dead. He was a worrier, and something connected with his job was preying on his mind. He was very much the introvert, and the reader may remember how sorely he took his rejection by the Army in 1914. Under the strain of things he developed brain fever. It was something that could be put right nowadays by modern treatment. Then there was no treatment. His heart failed, and that was that.

In the county service there was no pension, and Father had not taken the chance to become a volunatry contributor to the national scheme. He left under a thousand pounds, and there was no income. Lex had applied for, and obtained, a student assistantship in Plantation Street Church on the south side of Glasgow. I put an advertisement in the *Paisley Daily Express* offering my services as a tutor of backward children. Success was beyond my wildest dreams. I had not known there were so many backward children in Paisley.

One reply was from a lady who ran a small private school for the sons and daughters of the Paisley aristocracy, who went to be prepared for their entrance examination to prep school. She wanted someone to teach Latin. I was perfectly prepared to teach mathematics as long as I could keep a page ahead of the pupil in the textbook.

I got along famously in Fairhill School, and the pupils must have taken home golden opinions of the brilliant and handsome young teacher. Requests came in from the big houses, seeking my services to coach older children in a variety of subjects, all of which I had at least heard of. These were youngsters who were nervous about their entrance exam to public schools. Some of them had very good cause to be.

I found that I had some aptitude for teaching, and my pupils had their successes. Though there were failures too, like one little perisher who lived in a mansion. His mother, when she engaged me, informed me that corporal punishment was something she frowned upon. After five minutes with her son I realized the profundity of Solomon's advice that he that spareth the rod hateth his son.

We did our lessons in the billiards room, and all he wanted to do was throw the balls round the table, and, after the maid had brought up the afternoon tea, go into the garden and practise drop kicks. Although I was perfectly capable of teaching him both football and snooker, I was conscientious enough not to lose sight of the fact that I was being paid generously to prepare him for entrance to a public school, where his mother's attitude to corporal punishment would be laughed to scorn. I worked really hard, feeling that the sooner he got there the better. But there is a limit, and I reached it. I told him that if he had not done the prescribed work for the next day I would knock seven bells out of him. He did not and I did.

On my next visit the butler (it was that kind of a house) bade me to the presence. He did not stop and silently grip my hand. He just looked sympathetic. He, too, had suffered. Mother said that if I was to continue in her employment I would have to take a solemn oath that I would not again raise my hand to the son and heir. I told her that I could not in honesty give this undertaking, and I was dismissed, though without a stain on my character. The father was waiting for me in the hall. He thanked me, and gave me a fiver. I think he must have been wanting for years to do what I had done.

And so we managed to keep the household going, and in due course the university course finished.

D

18. My First Sermon

Just before this I met Margaret at a school dance. We began to go out occasionally together, though it took quite a time to reach that stage, and even longer to be introduced to her family. There had been other loves of a temporary nature during schooldays, but nothing serious. This turned out to be serious and permanent. In 1973 we celebrated our fortieth aniversary.

It was at this time, too, that I preached my first sermon.

In university there was a missionary society of which Lex was secretary. The idea was that if a church wanted 'supply', a student would go on behalf of the society and a collection would be taken for its funds. It was a moot point whether such a collection was better taken before rather than after the sermon.

Lex was a student short one weekend and asked me if I would stand in. The church was Sheuchan, Stranraer, and if they ever get round to writing the history of that church I hope that there may be mention of the fact that there Dow preached his first sermon.

The text was a simple one: 'What is man?' I reckoned that I could manage to answer the question satisfactorily in the statutory twenty minutes. After forty years of trying to find the answer I am still looking for it.

Pulpit supply was a bit chancy, however, and I decided to reply to an advert seeking a student assistant for the Union Church on the south side of Glasgow. I got the job at ten pounds a month, which was not at all bad, considering this was about as much as a tradesman got for a fifty-six-hour week, if he was lucky enough to be working at all.

Payment for pulpit supply was thirty-five shillings if the church you were supplying paid their minister the minimum stipend, which in those days was three hundred a year. For each ten pounds over the minimum which they paid in stipend, the supplier got another shilling. In other words, if the stipend was four hundred a year, the supplier got forty-five shillings. Which was quite an item.

In the normal way, two sermons did you, unless you were asked back. You preached them so often you could do it in your sleep, at the risk of preaching them in other people's sleep. My two were of a dramatic sort: one being an account of the trials, real and imaginary, of St Paul, the other dealing with some of the hills of the Bible.

There is a book called *The Life of a Scottish Probationer* which treats of the trials and tribulations of a newly licensed student looking for his first charge. There is a tale or two I could add to it. Like the time I was sent to Alva.

When I got off the bus I looked round for what we Scots, in our roundabout way, call a 'convenience'. The trouble with them is that civic authorities, with exemplary Scottish modesty, never place them where they are convenient. I could find none, and didn't like to ask a stranger. However, I did find my lodgings and was made warmly welcome by the session clerk. There was a grand fire, the table was generously spread, and, when his wife had been apprised of my arrival and introduced, there emanated from the scullery the reassuring aroma of the traditional ham and eggs. I still yearned, nay, my soul fainted, for that public convenience, and though I knew that they almost certainly would have a private one, I was young and shy, and didn't like to ask.

Given time and opportunity I knew I would enjoy the ham and eggs, though I had grave doubts of my capacity for any more liquid. The session clerk asked me if I was quite comfortable. This, again, is the roundabout way of the Scot. I was supremely comfortable, except for the one thing. Finally I had to ask. Obviously he had been wondering when I would ask. It was nearly too late.

I never pass through the Lanarkshire village of Harthill without breathing a reminiscent sigh. This was a Sunday-alone supply. If you were within travelling distance of Glasgow there was no week-end hospitality. I got there in good time, though the fare and a Sunday paper cost me, literally, my last penny.

I had a pleasant day. St Paul was in good form in the morning, and thereafter I enjoyed a substantial meal at a substantial farm, and went for a walk in the afternoon with the farmer's two substantial daughters. In the evening the mountains of the Bible were scaled without a hitch, though the thought did occur to me that possibly the subject was ill-chosen in that land of coal bings.

After evening service the congregation departed for their firesides and I awaited the arrival of the treasurer, for the pulpit supply regulations laid it down that the preacher had to be paid on the day. The treasurer came round to the vestry, made favourable comment on my ministrations, and handed me an envelope.

At the bus-stop I opened the envelope to extract the money for my fare and discovered that it contained a crossed cheque for two pounds fifteen.

Inexperienced as I was in the ways of the world I knew that it was highly unlikely that a bus conductress would give me a single ticket to Glasgow and change of a cheque for two pounds fifteen. But luck had not deserted me.

A youngish chap, obviously on his way to the pit, spoke to me and said he had enjoyed my children's address in the morning. This kind of thing is always happening. They never remember the sermon: just the children's address. I explained my predicament. He said he would pay my fare. I didn't want to impose on his generosity by telling him I still had to get to Paisley and that I didn't have the price of the fare from Glasgow, so I walked the seven miles, though I doubt if that road had ever been walked at that time of night by a young man wearing a bowler hat, suède gloves and a hallelujah collar, carrying an umbrella.

In Rothesay I had an alarming experience: my mind went blank. This had been known to happen before and it has happened since. But this was at a very awkward time: just before the benediction. I had done all sorts of things wrong during that service, including the omission of the Lord's Prayer. But there the congregation were, standing, heads bowed, waiting for the benediction, and possibly thankful that the service had reached that point. And I couldn't think how the benediction began. Cold sweat broke out on the brow. Then came the inspiration of desperation.

I said: 'Let us pray,' and began the Lord's Prayer; the congregation joined in, and when the prayer finished I went straight into the benediction with no hesitation. But that was not the end of it.

After service two of the elders came round to the vestry in the kindly way that Scots elders have, and, after expressing appreciation of the service, said they considered my way of ending the service to be as appropriate as it was unusual. They even wondered why nobody had thought of doing this before.

Being an honest kind of chap, I explained the circumstances, but I don't think they quite believed me. They just thought I was being modest.

I know ministers who are so terrified that they will get the petitions of the Lord's Prayer out of order that they have the words pasted on the bookboard in front of them. But this is not necessary, and I commend my method to any young minister who has a friend misguided enough to make him a present of this book.

Don't lead the prayer; just start it, then fade out when the voices of the congregation join in. And let the congregation take their time, as they always do, from the youngest child who is there. Children don't mutter or mumble the prayer. Their voices are as clear as bells. Isaiah said: 'And a little child shall lead them.' As usual, Isaiah was right.

Different ships, different long splices; and I don't think that any minister has the authority to tell other ministers how to do their job. From the start of my ministry I have always written out my sermons in full, taken the script into the pulpit, and followed it. My oldest friend in the ministry, George Boyd of St Andrew's, Ayr, does the same. Only he thereafter memorizes his sermon. I do not. This suits me; the other way suits George. The important thing is that we get everything down on paper.

It is different with prayers. I have tried written prayers, and I've tried memorized prayers. But for me they just don't feel right. And again this is not in the slightest criticism of those who prefer to do otherwise. The only prayers I ever wrote and read were when I was moderator of Greenock Presbytery, and when I've been conducting a service on radio or television.

One friend of mine was visiting an old chap who was ill and who was just about stone deaf. He said they would have a word of prayer. The wife said: 'But Archie will never hear you.'

To which my friend replied: 'It's no' Archie I'm speaking to.'

The effectiveness of prayer depends almost entirely on how

well a man knows his congregation. A congregation has a spirit
and prayer is a communication between that spirit and the spirit
which is God. If a congregation is what a congregation ought to
be, each one knows to whom the minister is referring in his intercessory prayer. If there's any doubt about that, he should refer to
the person by name. And in the pulpit you feel the spirit of the congregation mobilizing, and reaching out, and making contact.

When I was visiting people who were ill at home or in hospital, or
people who'd had a bereavement, I would say to them: 'You know
that the prayer of intercession on Sunday comes on at about half
past eleven. You've often joined in that prayer and thought about
other folk who were going through what you're going through. It's
you we'll be thinking about on Sunday. Remember that, and you'll
feel our thoughts reaching you.'

Broadcast prayers are different in one way, and yet not different
as long as the man who's leading the prayer doesn't generalize
and so become vague. The prayer for everybody can very easily
become the prayer for nobody. He shouldn't think on people.
He should think on persons: particular persons, and their needs
and their troubles. And at once the people who are listening begin
to think of other persons whom they know, and they wonder how
the man who is leading the prayer could know them too.

19. Learning the Trade

I went up to Trinity College, Glasgow, in 1928 to learn my trade. I was twenty years old. It was a big class, for classes were big at that time. This was the depression, and parents of any lad who seemed to have some scholastic ability were determined that he would not go into a trade. There was no future in the trades. He had to have a profession.

So up they went to university and eventually graduated and applied for admission to teacher training college, and they couldn't all get in. Some decided to make the best of a bad job (or to make the worst of a good job) and enter divinity college.

Hanging on my study wall is our year club photograph. There are forty-two of us in it, and this was just the old United Free Church side. The Auld Kirk students at university were additional to that. There must have been at least seventy between the two.

I lost that first year, not through illness or anything of the sort, but through inability to make head or tail of the Hebrew language. I was naturally sorry about this at the time, but not now. I would have finished at the age of twenty-three, which is too young. I still had too much to learn, and I don't mean just Hebrew.

By 1929 I was student assistant to a redoubtable man, T. Struthers Symington, on the south side of Glasgow. The Union Church had been set up by the old UF Church Presbytery of Glasgow as their big Home Mission experiment, and it was worked by Symington, the Bible Woman, Miss Ferguson, and a series of student assistants, myself being, I think, the last one.

Some idea of the work involved may be surmised if I give a few facts and figures. The congregation would number about a thousand, the Sunday Schools the same, the Women's Meeting four hundred, and the Bible class thirteen hundred. This seems unbelievable, but I have a photograph to prove it.

Two of the better-off churches, Sherbrooke and Camphill, took a lively interest in the work, with elders acting as assessors, and supplying teachers, leaders, and dispensers of tea at the Women's Meeting.

This is the kind of thing which West End churches miss today, now that Mission has become rather a dirty word. They have plenty of people willing to do something and with knowledge and training, but they haven't got enough to do. The East End churches have plenty to do, but not enough people with the knowledge and training to do it properly.

My main duty, apart from conducting occasional services, was to visit absentees from the Bible class. Each member of the class had a number, and three of us sat in the vestibule of the church with sheets bearing the numbers one to fifteen hundred. Each member coming in, gave his or her number to one of the three, who ticked it off on the sheet. When the class started I took the three sheets to the vestry and transferred all the ticks to one sheet. Then I marked the roll. This took about an hour.

After the class was over, Symington joined me, and we went over the roll together, picking out the names and addresses of all who had been absent for two successive Sundays, unless it was known that they were in hospital or jail or had emigrated. I had to visit them before next Sunday and report. This would entail about a hundred visits a week, and since all persons connected with the church live in the top flat, I reckon that in my three years in the Union Church I climbed Everest at least twice.

Being young and innocent it never struck me that some lassie in the Bible class would stay off deliberately so that she would get a visit from me. But Symington was neither young nor innocent.

'Ah yes,' he would grunt. (He was an enormous man with shoulders that would have terrified the All Blacks.) 'Here's Annie again, Pollock Street. Two off, one on, two off. I'll take that one, Dow.' Thereafter Annie's attendance improved.

The south side of Glasgow from Paisley Road Toll to Eglinton Street was not one of Glasgow's better residential areas, except for one or two streets of good tenements.

Centre Street had back-to-back tenements. The landlords at some time had decided that to have back greens was a waste of valuable space, so they built another row, and made pends in the front row to give access. Between, there were no lights, and the lights on the stairs were just gas jets.

On one occasion I was feeling my way across the narrow court between the blocks when I heard the sound of a scuffle and a girl's voice raised in what I assumed to be a cry for aid. Bracing my shoulders and swallowing the lump in my throat, I charged to the rescue, feeling like Sir Galahad. Reaching the scene of the affray I found my head being introduced to a window-sill. The cruel blow was not that, however. It was the fact that it was the girl who did it.

There was the time, too, when I had managed to raise the price of a spring outfit. At that time a fifty-shilling suit cost two pounds ten. But that was, after all, a week's pay. This is the mistake people make when they compare today's prices with those of forty years ago. The only proper comparison is between what could be bought for an hour's wage then, and what can be bought for an hour's wage now.

Anyway I was feeling very smart in my new suit and light grey snap-brim hat. In the course of my visitation I ascended the stairs of a close in West Street.

By this time I knew that it was pointless to spend time knocking on the door of the stairhead toilet, and asking if there was anyone at home. You either got no reply or it embarrassed the person inside. Occasionally you got a reply which embarrassed yourself.

In West Street the houses had once been substantial, but over the years had been divided and sub-divided. Each door had a cast-iron ticket on it indicating how many cubic feet of air it contained. Sometimes there was only one cast-iron sink on the landing to serve half a dozen houses.

I made my way to the top flat almost instinctively. I knocked, and a very large woman answered. With a beard, she would have done for Falstaff. She surveyed me from the snappy snap brim to the highly polished shoes. Her eyebrows went up.

What I should have said was: 'I am from the Union Church Bible class; we have noted from our records that Mary has been absent for two Sundays, and we are concerned in case there is something wrong.' Instead, and like a silly ass, I merely said: 'Is Mary in?' You should have heard what I got.

It appeared that Mary was indeed in, but that she was not in to the likes of me. It was me and my like who were the downfall of respectable girls like Mary, and I ought to think black burning shame. And the door was shut. I never told Symington about that one.

Nowadays the powers-that-be discourage, if they don't actually forbid, student assistantships, and they may be right. It is a shorter course, which leaves time for a compulsory assistantship after the student has been licensed. But in my day six years without grant and without earning anything was a long time.

By dropping student assistantships something may have been gained, but something has been lost. Most of the opportunities for assistantships were in the poorer East End churches where Home Board grants for assistance were available. Now, when a student is finished he goes to a better-off church which can pay him a reasonable salary. He is there not so much to help the minister as to learn the practical side of the job. I doubt, though, if he learns just as much about people as we did, and it is people that the job is all about. I may be wrong in this, of course.

Somehow, and for reasons which I won't specify, I don't think I would like to be a young minister nowadays. He must get many a sore heart. So did I, of course, in my day, but not just as many, I would think.

The church doesn't mean as much to people now as it did to the folk of churches like the Union Church. They didn't all live in slums, of course, and many of them were the salt of the earth. Slums is an unfair world. It isn't buildings that make a slum, it's people, as a great many socialist town councillors have found since slum clearance was started.

They had the idea, and I don't blame them for having it, that all you have to do to 'improve' people is to re-house them. This just isn't true.

The whole south side of Glasgow is demolished, as much of my first parish in the Townhead has been demolished. These areas were classed as slums. But my folk were not slum folk. They did not have a slum mentality. They lived there simply because they couldn't get a better house. They dressed well, and the girls on a Sunday were as much fashion-plate as any you would see in the West

End. How on earth a whole family managed to get washed at the one kitchen sink and get dressed in a room and kitchen house was a mystery to me, and for that matter still is.

The church was the place of sociability and of entertainment as well as of worship. For the others, the church was a place of light and warmth and brightness in a drab corner of Glasgow. A lot of tea was drunk, but there was something almost sacramental about it.

We had film shows on Saturday nights: silent films, of course. There was a full-size Pathé projector which Jim Harvie and I operated. Symington would go to the distributors, who would give him a quick run through a reel or two. He had strong views on what was to be seen and what was not. One week he couldn't make it and left the choice to the hirer.

The title was something innocuous like *Flames of Passion*. Jim and I put on the first reel. We weren't watching very carefully through the wee windows at the front of the box, and to us entered abruptly T. Struthers Symington, flaming with an entirely different kind of passion. It transpired that this was a film of a sort much commoner than is generally admitted by those who admire all things old, which depicted scenes not so much of what went on, but of what came off. He told us to speed it up; which we did.

Never in the course of romantic history has passion flamed so fast. We were knee-deep in celluloid by the time the reel finished. Fortunately the flames were not hot enough to set us on fire.

20. An Act of Giving

The Boys' Brigade Company of the Union Church was the 174 Glasgow; and a better company never went on parade. This was my introduction, as an old Boy Scout, to the BB. It was good that I was introduced to such a company as the 174.

It was run by two devoted brothers called Paterson, both bachelors, and the company was their life. They both held down fairly responsible jobs, but that was just to fill in time between parades.

The annual camp was held at Ardentinny, which was pretty well at the back of beyond. Harry Lauder used to sing of going over the hills to Ardentinny, just to see his bonnie Jeanie. Today's BB boy wants to camp at Blackpool or Bergen or places in between, with the result that the lads who've got money to spend are out of camp most of the time, spending it, while the others, who have spent their little all in the first week, just mope around for the second week. My experience is that the smaller the place the camp goes to, the better.

The people I've always admired are the wives of BB officers; and I suppose this is true, too, of the wives of Scouters. A man got a fortnight's holiday and he spent it at camp. His wife might be there too, in a special tent, but I don't think she enjoyed it much. Either that or she took a room at Rothesay, and I don't think she enjoyed that either. She was really the one who made the sacrifice. Margaret did it for years.

When I was in Greenock I got the Presbytery to write to the local industrialists asking them to give an extra week's holiday to leaders of organizations who were taking their boys to camp. We pointed out that when they were looking for apprentices they would take lads who were in the Scouts or the BB, and that they ought to encourage the men who provided them. The response was that this might cause discontent among their other workers. Which was nonsense. But this is the way industrialists think – if they think.

The result is that the voluntary worker is fast disappearing, and his place is being taken by the professional youth leader, many of whom (do not mistake me) are doing excellent work. But these are the leaders who are dedicated to the job, not to the pay. The uniformed organizations are finding it harder and harder to get their leaders.

I think on men like the Paterson brothers, and my old friends John Kerr, Scotland's greatest batsman, and Jim Swan: one the BB, the other the Scouts, who lived, ate and slept in their service. I doubt if we will see their like again.

I have written already of Sunday School trips. There never was one, and never will be one, like the Union Church trip: called Symington's Trip.

Every year he chartered the old Williamson Buchanan steamer, the *Eagle*, and sailed from the Bridge wharf to Lochgoilhead, where Glasgow Corporation had a public park. There were huts for eating in and facilities for cooking, and there were many heartburnings when the nights for selling the tickets came round.

The populace gathered in the large hall, sitting like the patients in a doctor's surgery. We were assembled in the lesser hall. Sitting at the middle of a long table was Symington, flanked by the secretaries of the various organizations for the young and for the old. I represented the Bible class, complete with roll book.

There was no fixed price for this excursion, though the economics of it would have done credit to any actuary. Those who had been faithful, and whose children had been faithful, were charged one price. On a sliding scale of infidelity, the others paid for their ticket.

And, of course, the minister (and his assistant, who was fast learning) knew the financial state of everyone present, and of some who were absent because of their financial condition. They were visited, given a ticket, and charged nothing at all. This loss had to be made up by despoiling the Philistines. Fortunately, or unfortunately, there were enough Philistines to compensate.

Those whose interest in Christianity rose and fell as the time of the trip approached or departed, would arrive before the bench, complete with the most elaborate and complicated reasons for their previous invisibility. They discovered, if they had not already known it, that so far as T. Struthers was concerned, the elaborate and the complicated are not necessarily convincing. I think that they were even having doubts about the innocence of the assistant.

They told tales of hardship that would have wrung the withers, but discovered that Symington, although he was as strong as a horse, had no withers to wring. The more they shot off their mouth, the more they paid through the nose.

The boat sailed early on the Saturday, and was always packed. The bar was closed for the day. Anyone who wanted to go 'down to see the engines', saw the engines, but tasted not. It was clearly understood that anyone seen entering or leaving the hotel at Lochgoilhead would walk home.

Down about Renfrew a small box of eatables was given to each passenger. This was to keep them going till we reached our destination, where a lunch box was distributed, containing, among other nourishing edibles, a pie.

The tea box, given out around five o'clock, contained a sausage roll, for a change. There remained one box for the way back, just in case any of the children didn't want to be sick on an empty stomach. It was quite a day. Symington could have organized the rations for the British Army.

A year or two before I went to Union Church there was the coal strike, and Williamson Buchanan told Symington that the trip would have to be off. He told them not to worry. If they provided the boat he would provide the fuel.

Special concessions were offered to purchasers of tickets. They could make up the difference by supplying anything that would burn. They brought coal, bundles of sticks, railway sleepers, firelighters, and anything that would raise steam. Expeditions were sent out to the well-to-do and well-inclined in the mansions of Pollockshields. Coal merchants were approached.

The stuff was collected in barrows, carried on shoulders, put in suitcases and brought on the green car. It was stored at the church and taken in carts to the Bridge wharf. With this assortment the *Eagle* was fired. No chief engineer had seen the like of it since David Niven went round the world in eighty days.

The *Eagle* got back around midnight. If it hadn't been that the tide was making she would never have made it at all. There was an almost imperceptible ripple at the bow, and it was rumoured that, at Finnieston, Symington made the supreme sacrifice by handing to the engineer his beloved pipe and bidding him put it on the fire.

Now and again I got the sharp side of his tongue; not so much for sins of commission as for sins of omission. I couldn't see the point in some of the jobs I had to do, and occasionally I said so.

He was a good preacher who could have been a lot better. He didn't give himself enough time to prepare. After one effort he admitted this, and I remarked that there's not much point in having the machinery well organized for getting people in, if you don't have anything worth saying to them when they are in. He could take this kind of criticism, and his usual reaction was to say: 'Right then, Dow, you take morning service on Sunday but pity help you if you spend the time writing a sermon when you should be visiting.'

One Sunday I preached on the text, 'I, if I be lifted up, will draw all men unto me.'

A minister can always tell when a sermon is getting across. Professor Macgregor used to say that when he was listening to a sermon he waited for 'the thrill'. Was it there or wasn't it?

That Sunday the thrill was there. This was the first time I had been aware of it. In the vestry afterwards Symington told me I had come closer to the heart of these tremendous words than anyone he had ever heard preach on that text. I never preached that sermon again. I was frightened that next time the thrill would not be there.

I was with Symington about a year and a half, then he left to go to South Beach and a quieter life. I couldn't see him having a quiet life anywhere. Or anybody else having a quiet life if he was around. A locum was appointed, whose main contribution to my education was to insist that I wore a hallelujah collar on Sundays. He left the work to Miss Ferguson and me.

After the vacancy was filled I stayed on for about a year, but it wasn't the same. Everything had centred on Symington. He had not delegated things to other people, and the whole thing fell away, which was a great pity, for it had been a remarkable achievement.

I was in my last year at college when I left Union Church in 1931 and committed myself once more to tutoring and pulpit supply. But I had learned a great deal from Symington on how to run a church and how not to. His advice was always practical.

I remember him once saying: 'There will come a time, Dow, when you have neglected a visit to one of your more difficult members. The longer you put it off, the harder it will be to go. But one day you will have to go, and you know it. Choose the filthiest night you can manage, ring the bell, and stand on the door mat with the water running off you. Nine times out of ten they will say: "Come away in, Mr Dow, fancy coming out to see us on a night like this".' It works too.

Although I was student assistant I had no official position as far as the courts of the church were concerned, but I was allowed to sit in on their discussions without taking part.

Once one chap uprose and said that if something or other was passed he would resign. Symington accepted the resignation on the spot.

We discussed the matter afterwards in the vestry. I asked him if he didn't think he had been a wee bit hard on the officebearer. He said I obviously didn't know that officebearer as well as he did. He advised me to take up the same attitude when I had officebearers of my own.

I hadn't been two months in my first charge, which was the Barony North in Castle Street, when I was faced with exactly the same situation. I was only twenty-four, and the officebearer was about seventy. He threatened to resign.

I swallowed the lump in my throat and asked him to send his resignation in writing to the session clerk. The letter never arrived. I learned later that he resigned about twice a year.

Then there was Mr Fletcher. He was an old chap who used to come to the prayer meeting on a Wednesday night. There aren't many prayer meetings in the Church of Scotland nowadays, and something has been lost which the church has never managed to replace. What he had been in his palmy days I don't know, but he must have been a man of some consequence. He spoke well, was always most polite, and dressed as immaculately as the condition of his clothes made possible. They were the best he could afford at jumble sales.

He wore a bowler hat of a slightly greenish hue. The coat would not have been out of place on an out-of-work tragedian. He always wore gloves and carried a walking stick with a silver band. He lived,

Above: Father and Mother
photographed in the parlour,
Greenlaw Avenue, 1912

Right: Myself when very young,
1911 or thereabouts

Left: Following my licensing, 1932

Below: Margaret and I married in April, 1933

Opposite above: Trinity College football team 1931–2. Willie Barclay is on my right in the front row

Opposite below: Union Church (south side) Bible Class, 1928

Opposite above: The Surma Valley
Light Horse takes a rest

Opposite below: Church parade
inspection, self nearest camera

Right: Camp cook, 1952

Below: Boys' Brigade camp, 1952,
at Angus MacVicar's Southend,
Kintyre. Tommy has the ball

Left: At work in the *Greenock Telegraph* office

Left below: Cartsburn Augustine Church Drama Group. *Bunty Pulls the Strings*, 1948

Left bottom: The Reeve's Tale (Colin Maclean) won the British Finals One Act Play competition, in 1956, for Greenock Players

Opposite above: The Life Boys, Cartsburn Augustine 1956

Opposite below: Cartsburn Augustine Kirk Session, 1959

Left: Presentation by producer Ray Linn Craig when we left for Arran in 1965. The picture is a scene from my own play, *Tailpiece,* which won the British Drama finals in 1962

Below: One of my two Arran churches, St Bride's, Lochranza, in the hollow of the hills

or existed, in the Rutland Model Lodging House at Paisley Road Toll.

Knowing, or suspecting, that I was a soft-hearted kind of chap, Symington had warned me of the blandishments of the hard-headed who live off the soft-hearted. Mr Fletcher was different. He was not a sponger, though he was prepared to do a 'touch'. But it was a carefully calculated touch. It was never more than I could afford and never less than he needed. One night it might be as little as a penny, but that was the difference between supper and no supper.

In Greenock I had quite a lot to do with the Trades Hotel, which was a very well-run establishment with good rooms and beds. Apart from working chaps who lodged there when they were on a job, and transport drivers and the like, twenty or thirty old men who had no relatives lived there and made it their home.

I was in the kitchen one day when one of the old fellows spoke through the hatch and asked: a bowl of broth, and was it dry out-side? I said that it had been when I came in and gave him his soup. He asked where the bread was. It was then I learned that a 'dry outside' is the heel of the loaf with no margarine on it.

Occasionally Mr Fletcher would ask for threepence, but not very often. He did not pretend that this was a loan which would be paid back. It was a financial deal between two gentlemen, one of whom was as embarrassed for a sixpence as the other was for a fiver. He did not wait behind every Wednesday night. Only now and again, or maybe usually.

One Wednesday he waited. We always began by discussing the theme of the service. I often wondered how relevant it was to him. While we talked I felt in my pocket for the few coins which reposed therein, feeling round the edge of the rare half-crown in case I might mistake it for a penny. He asked if I could oblige him with two shillings.

This was unheard-of. For a wild moment I thought he might be getting married. I said that this was quite a lot; was it for something special? In perfect seriousness he explained, and in perfect serious-ness I listened.

It appeared that I was going to leave the Union Church, and it had come to his notice that the regular attenders at the prayer meeting intended to make a small presentation to me. These regular attenders knew of the close relationship which existed between myself and himself, and he would not like them to get the impression that he was not grateful. He felt that nothing less than a donation of two shillings would indicate how high I stood in his esteem.

I handed him the florin, he handed it to the treasurer, making, I would think, the largest subscription. But it taught me a lesson I have never forgotten and never will.

In all acts of giving from those who have to those who have not there must be no embarrassment and no patronage.

21. Trinity College

With the university professors I'd had very little contact, except for the interview with Hetherington about the hat. In Trinity College, however, it was different, for we were much closer to the professors. They used to have lunch with us when it was their wife's washing day.

In my first year – the one I had to repeat – the meals were cooked by the janitor, Willie Cruikshanks. The menu did not vary much: one day sausages, the next day pies, then back to sausages again. Then Willie retired and was replaced by Norman Lamont and his charming wife who served coffee in the common room at eleven, which must have affected drastically the profits of Craig's tea room in Woodlands Road.

Professor Niven used to wander down there for a coffee from time to time. He was the last of our professors left alive, and died not so very long ago. One day George and I were in Craig's and Willie Niven entered and asked if he might join us. We were delighted. We talked of this and that, Willie's benign countenance reflecting no comment on some of the rather callow ideas we delivered ourselves of. As the hour approached, Willie began to consult his watch, plainly as a hint to us that it was time we got cracking for college.

When we made no move he said finally: 'Haven't you two got a class to go to?' We admitted that we had and told him whose class it was: one of the Old Kirk professors, some of whom were not all that popular with the old UF Kirk profs, of whom Willie Niven was one. Willie made no comment. He beckoned the waitress over and ordered three more coffees.

The two churches united in 1929 and there was a certain amount of duplication of teaching, and possibly of effort, until the classes which had started before then had completed their course, or until professors retired. We were with the old UF professors mostly.

W. M. Macgregor was, of course, Principal of Trinity, and a fine teacher of the New Testament, though lacking Willie Barclay's flair for putting it across. Willie Barclay was in my year, and is reckoned to be the most brilliant student to pass through the college. Barclay and I played in the football team, though he was just an ordinary player and I was captain. Here's a story that's typical of Willie.

In the last year, students had to prepare a New Testament exegesis, which is a full analysis and interpretation of a passage of Scripture. He is supposed to look up all the available manuscripts, and make his own translation of the Greek. He then writes down all the variants, which are the textual differences between one and the other. Having completed this useful and, no doubt, necessary task, he then examines carefully the background of the book, the authorship and the rest, and finishes with a homiletic expansion which, in plain language, is a sermon.

The idea is that after you qualify, you do this every week, twice. In college they gave you a year to do it once. Willie Macgregor handed out the passages one morning, and after class Willie Barclay asked me what I had got in the draw. I told him I'd got the second chapter of the Epistle to the Hebrews. There may have been a trace of gloom on my face. For next day my friend handed me a foolscap sheet with all the variants written on it. He said it hadn't taken him as long as it would have taken me. I wonder how he knew. I did not question the accuracy of them. He didn't make that kind of mistake.

Knowing that my exegesis had at least a good start, however it finished, I worked hard at it, trying to live up to the variants. There would be about a hundred pages of writing in it. And in due season I handed it in.

Some months later George and I were having coffee in the common room when Willie Macgregor entered, bearing in his hand a manuscript. I recognized it and told George so out of the corner of my mouth. He looked as anxious as he would have looked had it been his own.

Macgregor came with slow deliberate step and stood behind us, like a High Court judge returning to pass sentence after going out to find his black cap. The only sound was the tapping of the manuscript on his hand. There was no sound of heavy breathing. George and I were not breathing at all.

Macgregor reached forward a long arm and laid the document before me. In fear and trembling I hastily read the criticism written on the front page: 'An excellent piece of work, which I sustain with peculiar pleasure.'

That exegesis has long ago disappeared, but these words are graven on my heart.

With the departure of Willie Cruikshanks it was necessary to engage another cook, and the Senate this time decided to engage a graduate of the Domestic Science College, or Dough School. She was Cathie Gillespie, one of several daughters of the minister of Dundonald. Willie Barclay was appointed students' lunch convener. He was supposed to keep an eye on the cook, which he did to such good effect that after college was over and he was called to Trinity, Renfrew, he and Cathie were married, and still are.

I learned later that to succeed her they appointed a younger sister, who, in turn, married the next lunch convener. Whereupon the Senate decided to appoint someone of more mature years and fewer attractions.

The professor of Old Testament was John Edgar McFadyen, a great scholar and a great wee man. Occasionally before starting his lecture Johnnie would say: 'During my reading last night, gentlemen, I had an idea concerning the interpretation of a passage, which you might find an interesting sermon subject.'

He would then give the text and the suggested treatment, and the pencils would get busy, for Johnnie's ideas were so much fine gold. They say, though I will not vouch for this, that one Lanarkshire congregation, depending on student supply, got the same sermon for five successive Sundays from five different students.

A. J. Gossip was professor of Christian Ethics and Practical Training. He was a magnificent preacher, though sometimes in his lectures he got so carried away that he soared into space unknown, where it was very hard to follow him. It was all most inspiring, but there wasn't enough of the practical in the training. I came away from college (and this was not entirely my fault this time) with very little idea of the mechanics of the ministry.

I had already conducted many funerals from Union Church, of course. Death was a commonplace in the parish, and everyone came to Symington. During one flu epidemic I spent the afternoons at Craigton cemetery taking the committals while Symington stayed in the parish taking the services.

But all I knew of baptisms was what I had seen my own minister, or Symington, do. At the age of twenty-three I had never been to a wedding. All I knew about communion services was, again, what I had seen and heard done. I left college knowing very little more about these offices than I had known when I went there.

Of course it wouldn't be right for a man, be he professor or not, to lay down the law and say: 'You must do it this way.' After all, his way may not be the best or most seemly way. But in the sacraments there are essentials which must not be left out and which must not be changed. Nevertheless there must be some latitude of expression, though not of interpretation. I'll give one practical example.

It was shortly after I went to Greenock: that is 1943, and there was an officebearer I simply could not get on with, try though I did. The first time I visited him he said: 'I could tell you something about everybody in that kirk,' He would have, too, if I had encouraged him.

I didn't know what to do, for I don't like not getting on with people. Things went from bad to worse, and then communion Sunday came round. At the table he was sitting at my side, and I knew that, as things were between us, this sacrament was meaningless to me, whatever it was to him. I wanted to offer him my hand, but knew that everyone would notice, for most of them knew how things were.

While the elements were going out to the congregation I sat thinking. How was I to make the gesture without making a spectacle of it? Then I remembered one of Chesterton's Father Brown stories: the one about the broken sword which would prove that the general was a murderer and traitor. Father Brown thinks: 'Where do you hide a pebble? On the beach. Where do you hide a leaf? In the forest. Where do you hide a sword? On the battlefield.'

When the sacrament was over, and before we sang the last hymn, I said to the congregation that this was an appropriate time to show our fellowship with one another. We would each shake hands with those sitting on our right and our left. I offered him my hand and he took it. But it didn't make any difference, and by next communion season he had left the church. This time I ommitted the ceremonial handshaking, and after the service the elders asked me why, and to bring it back. It has been a permanent part of the communion service for me ever since. People like it, and, after all, how often does a man shake hands with his wife, or a son shake hands with his mother, except at New Year.

A. B. Macaulay was professor of Apologetics and Dogmatics, and it took me some time to decide which was which. A. B. was a kindly soul, though not all that great as a lecturer. Fortunately he handed out duplicated sheets giving a digest of his lectures, but he still insisted that we attended them.

Then there was Professor J. Y. Simpson, nephew, I think, of the discoverer of chloroform as an anaesthetic. Some of his lectures had the same effect. Someone at some time had decided that students for the ministry should know something about science. That must have been at the time when science and theology were fighting a bitter battle of words. Simpson's chair of Natural Science had been founded. Round J.Y.'s class there were shelves and cases with jars of specimens like the things the witches put in Macbeth's stew. These were used to dress the top table at the Christmas dinner.

We had to take elocution for a couple of years as well. I remember Willie Barclay telling me that one of the profs (an Old Kirk one) had taken him aside and told him that he would never have any advancement in the church unless he got rid of his Glasgow accent.

Willie was quite indignant. It's a Motherwell accent he has. The odd thing is that Willie with his Motherwell accent, and myself with my Paisley accent, are at least among the top ten in religious broadcasting in Scotland. There must be a moral in this somewhere.

The first elocution teacher I served under was a chap called Bruce Alston, who must have been on the stage at some time or another. He was drama personified, with a range of gestures like a Boy Scout doing semaphore signalling.

I have never mastered gesture, though I have been an amateur actor for a long time now. I'm far more comfortable in the pulpit with both my hands stuffed into my cassock pockets. I'm glad somebody invented the cassock. You don't have suddenly to worry in case your front buttons aren't properly fastened.

There was a terribly embarrassing moment for me in the Union Church at the Women's Meeting, which was held in the afternoon, and which I had to chair after Symington left. (The locum always seemed to have something on when the Women's Meeting was arranged.)

Behind the platform of the hall there were the waiting rooms, with the usual offices, and the lady who was to sing had retired to the appropriate one just before the proceedings commenced. She joined me on the platform and the proceedings began. The moment arrived for me to introduce the vocalist, who would weigh, at a rough estimate, some twelve stone.

She uprose from her seat by my side, and stepped to the front of the platform, and I saw to my horror that when she had been readjusting her clothing after having been where she had been, she had got the tail of her frock tangled with the elastic on top of the necessary and useful garment underneath. She delivered herself of her song, which was well received, and prepared for the encore, which is always given, whether the first one has been well received or not. All was well, as long as she was facing the audience, but what on earth was going to happen when she turned round to resume her seat? It would have been like the launch of the *Queen Mary*.

When she completed the encore and was bowing to the applause I stepped forward, clapping enthusiastically, clapped her on the shoulder with my right hand, and with my left managed to extricate the garment. Fortunately the elastic did not snap.

Bruce Alston greatly admired my voice, though years later it was described by William Hickey in the *Scottish Daily Express* as being reminiscent of the sound made by celery passing through a mincer. I recited *Kubla Khan* for him before the class and he nearly burst into tears. It seems that he had never heard it done better and that Coleridge must be applauding from the spirit world. But it also seems that it ought not to be done with the hands in the pockets. He indicated the appropriate gestures which I tried vainly to emulate, but found that although I could get the hand up all right with the forefinger pointing heavenward I could never figure out how to get it down again. And you cannot spend twenty minutes of a sermon giving an imitation, however convincing, of the statue of Liberty.

Symington went in for gesture a bit. One Sunday he came away with a magnificent one, and his detachable cuff shot off. This was bad enough in an eloquent moment which was calculated to have the congregation glued to their seats. But the beadle, who was an unimaginative sort, retrieved it from the front stalls, and took it back up the pulpit steps and handed it over to its owner. It rather took away from the effect.

In that dreadful moment I made a vow. I did not make a vow that I would never make gestures. I just made a vow that I would never wear detachable cuffs.

In our last year George was instrumental in having May Watt empanelled as an elocution teacher. She was, I think, an original member of the Scottish National Players along with my old friend Jamieson Clark. If I'm dating May too far back, I apologize. But not to Jamie. Nobody could date him too far back.

May turned up one Sunday night in the Union Church when I was preaching, to learn how her elocution classes were affecting me, and when May turned up it was indeed a turn up. When she took her place in the middle of the front gallery it was like Bette Davis taking over the Tent Hall. I was the talk of the Bible class for weeks.

They ought to have known better, for by this time Margaret and I were going steady, and she was often at services in the Union Church.

Degree examination results appeared in the *Glasgow Herald*, and I knew that the geology results would be in on the Monday. It was Sunday morning when I got in touch with them by way of a phone box. We did not have a telephone. I asked the chap who answered if he would look up the geology results and tell me the best or the worst. He was not all that anxious, but he did, and told me that I had passed. I was now a Master of Arts; a triumph of perseverance over natural limitations.

So the college course, like everything else, came to an end, and what is an end but a beginning? It was 1932, and the course was run; by no means a distinguished one, or covered as swiftly as it might have been, but, nevertheless, run. We were taken on trials for licence, and then went forth to learn our job.

Lex and I were licensed together in the Paisley Abbey, and it was a very proud day for our mother and sister, and for Margaret and Marion, my brother's future wife, now, alas, dead.

Having toiled for most of his student days in Plantation Street, Lex felt that his vocation lay in this kind of work, and volunteered his services to the Home Board, who placed him in the mining village of Kelty in Fife, and thither he went with Mother and Elsie, which meant the break-up of our old home in Paisley. I thought that this was a mistake, but did not raise my voice in protest.

After all, Mother, at very considerable sacrifice, had put two of us through university, and Elsie through Paisley Grammar. She was entitled, for however short a time, to be the Lady of the Manse. But it meant that I, with no visible means of support, had to go into lodgings in Paisley. For the first and last time in my life I was served with a cooked breakfast in my room.

This cost me thirty shillings a week, which did not leave very much over from a pulpit supply fee. Though I will say for the clerk of Supply, whose son had been in college with me, that he did pretty well by me. Sometimes we went to the pictures on a Friday night when Margaret got her pay, and the family fed me well too. They must have thought that Margaret had prospects or that I had possibilities.

Of course I went through to Kelty for Lex's induction, and delivered myself of a speech. What the subject was I do not know. Lex probably. I stayed for a day or two (it was cheaper) and became quite pally with the chap next door who was a shot firer in the Kelty Jewel pit. One day he said to me: 'You know, Mr Dow, it's an ill-divided world. There's your brother with three hundred pounds a year, and here I am with no more than six pounds a week.'

As soon as Lex and I were licensed, Mother took us to Smart and Rolland, the accepted Paisley tailor, and had us rigged up in ministerial frock-coats, complete with tile hats. The first day we wore them it caused quite a sensation in Mavisbank Terrace.

Anyway, I had to get a job. But if you'd been brought up in the old

UF Church you knew that there was something rather *infra dig.* in replying to advertisements from churches who were looking for a minister. And sending testimonials.

Apart from anything else, I didn't have any testimonials. I might have asked Willie Macgregor for one, though I believe that on one occasion when asked to supply a testimonial he had replied that Mr So-and-so had been a very ordinary student and would probably turn out to be a very ordinary minister. I doubt if he would have given me that kind of testimonial.

The best he could have done would have been to say that I had once written an exegesis which he had sustained with peculiar pleasure, and that I sang 'A Jovial Monk' rather well. It wasn't worth the risk. But only old parish church students and ministers replied to adversitements. For us UF students the ministry was a vocation. So that when you heard that a charge was vacant you just pulled as many strings as possible.

It so happened that in the early summer of 1932 my home minister, Lewis Sutherland, happened to be talking to another minister who was interim moderator in the Barony North Church of Glasgow, just opposite the Royal Infirmary. They had heard one or two men, but opinion was divided. Sutherland mentioned my name, and I was asked (not very hopefully, I would imagine) to preach in the vacancy. St Paul was in good form in the morning, and the mountains of the Bible did not let me down in the evening. They had a meeting some days later, and I was called.

Before me as I write are two of the relics of the past which I treasure. Gone are the lecture books and the essay books, and even the celebrated exegesis. There are a few football teams, but that is all, except for these two.

One is the Bible presented to me by the Presbytery of Paisley at our licensing. That was 22 March 1932. The other is the programme of my ordination and induction on 20 October in the same year. On the front is the picture of a young man wearing a clerical collar that looks far too big for him, and with his hair parted in the middle. It is still parted in the middle, though the parting is now considerably wider.

There were presentations of robes and the rest; there were speeches, including one by Lachlan Maclean Watt of Glasgow Cathedral,

who got so carried away that he abandoned the English and returned
to his native Gaelic.

The lads of the college were there too; all now with the title
Reverend before their names: George Boyd, Willie Barclay, Lauren
Macdougall and Algy Gordon. The votes of thanks were called for
by Willie's father, who had given me a lot of good advice.

Lewis Sutherland and Struthers Symington preached at the
introductory services: I took the evening service. My text was:
'The Jews require a sign, and the Greeks seek after wisdom; but
we preach Christ crucified, unto the Jews a stumbling block, and
unto the Greeks, foolishness, but to them which are called, both
Jews and Greeks, Christ, the power of God and the wisdom of
God.'

When I was shaking hands with the departing congregation one
old chap had a few words to say. He told me I was better-looking
than my photograph; something, I assure you, which was not at
all difficult to accomplish. Then he said: 'I thought for a while
you'd get lost among thae Jews and Greeks, but ye cam' tae the
Christ in guid time.'

I refrained from telling him that I'd been getting lost among these
Jews and Greeks for the last three years, or at least among the
pitfalls of their languages. But I hope that, after forty years, I have
never got very far away from the Christ.

On the day of my ordination and induction Margaret and I
became engaged. I had bought the ring without consulting her. I
thought the least I could do was buy it in David Dow's the Jeweller.
I told them my name but they offered no discount. It cost ten pounds.

22. Barony North

Perhaps I made a mistake in going to Barony North, but after all it was the first offer I had; you've got to earn a living somewhere and somehow, and there was no one to advise me. But a man of twenty-four, not dry behind the ears yet, wanting to get married as soon as possible, is inclined to take the first chance that comes his way. He is also still convinced that there is such a thing as a 'call', and that the reason why this offer has come his way is that it was ordained that it should come his way.

But Barony North was too big a job for a man of my years. Maybe that is wrong. Maybe there are others who could have made a better job of it than I did. I don't know.

This is not to say that I made a bad job of it: anything but. I've still many friends out of Barony North, though they're all getting on a bit now, and there's some of them think I was the best minister that church ever had. This is because they were about the same age then as I was when I became their minister. But there was so much to learn.

By this time Lex was married, which meant of course that Mother and Elsie had to find a place. Naturally, they found a place in the Barony North manse in Westercraigs, Dennistoun. It was quite a mansion, complete with a Swiss-type turret with a small room at the top which was quite useless for anything but an observation post, and there is more or less nothing to observe in Dennistoun.

Mother had now become in a position beyond her wildest dreams. She was lady of the manse for the second time.

The manse was furnished sketchily, and mostly from the remains of the Mavisbank furniture which had been put in store. But Mavisbank had had a kitchen and a parlour, two downstairs bedrooms and two attic bedrooms. There were also pots and pans and other necessities. We got by all right, and, of course, Mother was a first-

class manager. The trouble was that I was supposed to be saving
up to get married, and when all the bills were paid there was nothing
left to get married on.

Barony North was the old Barony Free Kirk, and the Free Kirk
had their own way of paying the stipend. I suppose it was a way
which ensured that the minister got his stipend, but it was a bit
awkward too for a young fellow starting out.

Old United Presbyterian churches were different. When a minister
was inducted the treasurer handed him a quarter's stipend in advance.
In the old Free Kirk £150 of your stipend was paid quarterly in
arrears. and three months is a long time to wait when you have
absolutely nothing behind you. I never had a bank account, and
sometimes I wish that I still hadn't when I look at it.

The Church of Scotland had a useful provision for young ministers. You could get a loan of a hundred pounds to be repaid over
ten years, without interest, to furnish your manse. And a hundred
pounds went a long way in 1932. But I had more than the minimum
stipend, which in those days was £300 a year. I did not qualify.

But Margaret and I decided to get married in 1933, and depend on
wedding presents and the hire-purchase system to get set up. As a
consequence we placed a millstone round our neck from which,
even yet, we have not fully recovered. As many a young couple in
the ministry, and not in the ministry, will well understand.

In April we were married with much pomp and ceremony, and
departed to Pitlochry on our honeymoon with something like five
pounds between us. That lasted us the better part of a week, then
we came home and got on with the work.

It was harder for her than it was for me. I had been to college
where I had not learned a great deal that was of very much use to
me, but she had seen church life only from the outside, as Sunday
School teacher, and pourer out of tea at ecclesiastical functions.
Now she had to take charge of a Women's Guild and a Women's
Meeting and other delights, as well as entertaining a steady stream
of callers at the manse. She made a grand job of it. In fact I think
that the congregation as a whole thought more of her than they did
of me.

Barony North had a parish which was not unlike the south side of Glasgow where I had served my apprenticeship, but most of the members did not live in the parish. They lived all over the city of Glasgow, but mainly in the better residential district of Dennistoun. Visitation was a real problem.

I had no car: very few ministers had cars in those days. I had to depend on the tram-car, and that takes some time getting from one place to another. A funeral was a whole afternoon, by the time I got to the house and got back again, and there were quite a number of funerals. I spent a great deal of my time with the youth organizations, notably the Boys' Brigade, the 110 Glasgow, with a group of first-class officers who all became my close friends, and who still are, though many of them I haven't seen for a long time.

There was also a Junior Choir and we indulged in such extravaganzas as *The Dragon of Tangly Mountain.* I never saw a dragon getting into such a tangle as that one did.

Barony North had a football team, too, struggling in the second division of the Glasgow Churches League. I signed on. We played on an ash pitch off Alexandra Parade, and to play at all in the Glasgow Churches League was taking your life in your hands.

I remember one game: I think it was against Hood Memorial. I was playing right half, and their inside left was taking the mickey out of me. Many of his remarks, for he kept up a kind of running commentary, were couched in language which was very much out of place in the Churches League. At half-time our captain took their captain aside, and explained that Barony North's right half was the minister. The second half was a complete transformation. The inside left would bring the ball up to me and then stand back so that I could get a kick at it.

Later on my old friend George Boyd was called to Dennistoun Parish. He had spoken at my induction and I was invited to retaliate. Dennistoun Parish team could have beaten a lot of junior teams and were always top of the first division of the Churches League. They had a splendid enclosed ground at the top of Meadowpark Street. In the course of my remarks I challenged them to play Barony North, if George would play for them. He was a first-class player. In due course and after much advertising, and before packed terraces, the game was played. We drew, nothing all.

After the game one of my members told me that he had been

standing with a couple of strangers. One asked who the two ministers
were. The other said: 'I don't know. They're all playing like ministers.'

About the same time the Glasgow Ministers' football team was
formed. I can't remember all who were in it. Leonard Small was
in goal: there was Alpine Munro, and Arthur Gray and Jimmy
Cottar who had played rugby for Scotland. Other names have
slipped my mind. We played at Cathkin. One night we played the
Glasgow Sporting Press. George and I were picked right and left
back respectively. Willie West, a first division referee, was in charge
and we knew that his decisions would be informed.

George and I decided to save our legs and play the offside game.
We had such success (we won, by the way) that the report in the
papers said: 'Dow and Boyd showed a good understanding of the
game.'

Another ministerial venture in Glasgow was the concert party.
George Macleod was in Govan at the time and he wanted funds to
run schemes he was trying for the unemployed men of the place.
And there were plenty of them. To raise funds, the Glasgow ministers' Concert Party was brought together. I was one of them.

There was Alex Stewart and Harry Law and Jimmy Macmore-
land, and Jimmy Haddow (who was a first-class conjurer), John
Swan of the Ramshorn, Duncan Macpherson, Tom Brown, and
others. It wasn't a bad concert party. We toured churches and took
collections, but the big event was when we took the Lyric Theatre
for a week.

The sketches which we put on all had a church flavour. There
was the annual general meeting of the Beadles' Union, and the
annual general meeting of the congregation, complete with minister,
treasurer, session clerk, clerk to the board, leaders of organizations
and all the rest. Each night we had a notability as guest, who was
accommodated in one of the boxes. This night it was Lachlan
Maclean Watt of Glasgow Cathedral. All was going well till we
came to the sketch of the annual general meeting.

Jimmy Haddow was in the audience, which represented the congregation. His clerical collar was covered by a muffler, and he was
wearing a bonnet. He started to make interruptions. He continued
to make interruptions, until Lachlan Maclean Watt rose in his

wrath and called proceedings to a halt. He then told Jimmy what he
thought of him, in a mixture of English and Gaelic. Here was a
group of ministers giving up their valuable time and their talent
(he didn't say if that was valuable or not) to help unemployed men
like himself. Deserving cases who did not spend their money on
drink, as Jimmy had obviously been doing.

Jimmy stood with bowed head and took it all, and when Lachlan
had exhausted himself, Jimmy uncovered, and removed his muffler.
It was one of the funniest unrehearsed acts I have ever seen.

A young minister has to spend time in his study. He has no material
at his back. Well, I had. I had the trial of Paul and the mountains
of the Bible, but I'd used them already when I was preaching for
Barony North.

I doubt very much if the laymen realizes just how much work
and how much writing is involved in preparing two sermons for
each Sunday throughout the year. I didn't have two; I had three.

After I'd been in Barony for about a year a group of the youngest
members approached me: they were members over the Bible class
age. They asked if it would be possible to have discussion on a
Sunday night.

Our services were morning and afternoon, which, as I pointed
out in an earlier chapter, was the traditional Scottish way. So without
altering that arrangement I put on another service in the evening.
It didn't follow the traditional pattern, and the sermon subject
was always something discussable. I found the Adult Education
handbooks published by the Society of Friends very useful here.
But that took a lot of preparation too.

And there's always a certain amount that even a man has to do
in the house, especially when his wife's expecting her first baby.
We engaged a maid. In those days many manses, if not most manses,
had a maid, and May was a very good one. Her pay was three pounds
ten a month, with, of course, her keep, and she seemed very happy
with it.

Of course, all the wedding present china and silver and crystal
was still intact, and our table was quite a picture when we sat down
to our mince.

By this time Mother and Elsie had taken a house in Cardonald,
E

though we saw them often, as well as Margaret's two sisters, Sadie and Helen. She had a brother too, Bert. I had been his best man before we were married.

The baby was due in March 1934, and we engaged a midwife. It transpired that she was a Roman Catholic, but that made no difference. She was first-class at her job. I think her pay was three pounds a week, and we had her for about a month before and after.

Everything went well at the birth, and there were no complications except when the members of Margaret's family arrived. Sister Sadie would come almost every night from her work in Paisley, and always made sure to slam the door in case the baby was sleeping.

The baby was baptized by George Boyd, my oldest friend in the ministry, and was named Margaret Rodger Leslie Dow. We really should have called her Leslie, as her own first born is called, for when mother and daughter have the same name it must be 'old Margaret' and 'young Margaret'. Of course, if we'd called Margaret Leslie, she couldn't, for the same reason, have called her own daughter Leslie.

What so much inhibits the work of the church is money. It takes a lot of money to keep a kirk going, and what was soon discovered after the union of the churches in 1929 was that there were far too many of them.

Wherever there was an old parish church there was also an old Free Church which had broken away from it in 1843. Nine times out of ten there would also be an old UP Church. Three churches were doing the work which one could have done.

The old parish churches were well enough off with their endowments, and the Free and UP Churches had a strong nucleus of the middle class whose givings were generous to the point of sacrifice. They were independent, and they were prepared to pay for it. But with the passing years the middle-class folk tended to move away from the centre of the towns to the suburbs; and the suburban churches were prosperous enough. They were prepared to help the others financially. They supported foreign and home missions with exemplary liberality. But the East End churches became more and more working-class churches, and in the early thirties, with the best will in the world, they simply had not the money to keep things going.

This is where the frictions in congregational life begin, though I will say that in Barony North we had few frictions. But it gradually became borne in on me that in the very small area of the Townhead of Glasgow there were half a dozen of us struggling away simply to keep going, when the work could all have been done by two.

The Roman Catholic church does not, of course, have the same heritage of split and division. There must have been differences of opinion but they managed to preserve at least the appearance of solidarity. The result is that when they provide a church they provide just one church for a sizable parish, and staff it adequately with men whose different talents can be applied to different aspects of the job.

There is only one roof to keep in repair, and one beadle and one organist to pay, and the time is over when these officials were content to work for coppers. Beadles and organists, naturally, may approve of the continuation of the old system, but sheer force of economics must work the change eventually.

My generation, which was involved in the union of the churches, is fading from the scene, at least from the active scene, and our successors have no personal recollection or knowledge of the older ways. But it seems to me that maybe a chance was missed when the Old Kirk and the UF Kirk united in 1929. It is only a dream, of course, and it is far too late now.

But wouldn't it have been a good idea if there had been a 'general post' of ministers, with all the UF ministers going to former parish churches and all the parish ministers going to old UF churches? Then the UF ministers could have impressed on the old Parish Kirk members what their financial responsibilities were, and the old Parish ministers could have told the UF members who was boss.

It seems to me that one of the main differences between the two denominations was that in the UF Church you would get plenty of help in running things, along with a great deal of advice on how to do it. Whereas in the old Parish Kirk the minister would get a general blessing to do anything he liked so long as he did it himself.

There was something I learned early, and I learned it through Symington, though not at his instruction. Bulldozers had not been invented then, but he was one. The result was a lot of argument, and sometimes a deal of unnecessary unpleasantness. Ministers should not introduce new ideas; especially young ministers. It is better to have a quiet sociable chat with two or three office bearers and sell them an idea. They think it over, and talk about it among themselves. Then at some session or board meeting they introduce this idea as if it was their own. By this time they are quite convinced that it was their own idea in the first place. And the thing is done. It doesn't matter who does good, so long as good is done.

I've mentioned earlier the lack of practical training we had in college. The first couple I married lived in sin for the best part of a week till the registrar phoned me to tell me I had forgotten to get them to sign the schedule.

Then there was the couple who had arranged to be married in the manse one Friday night. Church weddings were unknown in those days, and morning suits and grey toppers were something they wore at Ascot. Marriages were in the manse, or in the vestry, or, if it was a big 'do', in the Co-operative Hall.

> A nice wee lass, a braw wee lass
> Is bonnie wee Jeanie McColl.
> I gied her my mother's engagement ring
> And a bonnie wee tartan shawl.
> I met her at a wedding in the Co-operative Hall,
> I was the best man and she was the belle of the ball.

This was true. I often think that if all the guests handed over to the young couple what it had cost them to hire the now necessary garments it would set them up for life.

Anyway, this couple turned up on the Friday night, complete with best man and bridesmaid. I asked them politely if they had the schedule. A blank look came across the four faces. What was the schedule I was asking for?

I explained that after they had had the banns cried, and taken the certificate to the registrar, he issued a schedule which had to be filled up and signed by the contracting parties, the witnesses, and the officiating clergyman. They had omitted to procure this essential document. I was in a bit of a quandary, being rather young at the game.

The bride-to-be burst into tears and the bridesmaid followed suit. The groom looked as if he was due to burst out greeting too. He explained that the relatives, friends and neighbours were waiting in the house for their return. I said I was sorry, but I simply could not do it. Then light broke on the face of the best man.

He said: 'I tell you what, Mr Dow. Could ye gie them something to dae them over the weekend and we'll come back on Monday?'

But being a Friday, the Glasgow registrars stayed open till half past seven. I packed them off in their taxi, and eventually all was well.

There was another time when Margaret and I were flat broke. This happened periodically, usually about the end of the quarter. But we hadn't the price of twenty Capstan between us. I told her that all would be well. It was Friday, and there was a wedding.

In the thirties book tokens were not common currency for presents for the minister; a box of hankies, an umbrella, a pair of gloves or even, on one occasion, a pair of hand-knitted socks, was the customary gift from members. Non-members tended to make a cash payment, which seldom, if ever, exceeded five shillings.

The couple turned up and were given full connubial honours. After the ceremony I showed them out as the butler might have done. The four of them went down the front steps and my heart fell. Then the best man came back up. My heart rose again.

He handed me a pound note. I nearly dropped. This was not unusual. This was unprecedented. I moistened my lips to be able to thank him. Then he spoiled it. He asked me if I had fifteen bob change. They may or may not have approved of free love, but they certainly got a free marriage.

So four years went past; four busy years, but four years in which I felt I wasn't really getting anywhere. Not that I was wanting to get anywhere in the way of advancement. I just felt that the job wasn't getting anywhere in particular. One day I looked at the advertisements in the *Glasgow Herald*: something, I assure you, that I was not in the habit of doing. The Colonial and Continental Committee were looking for a chaplain for the Scots tea planters in Assam. I asked Margaret if she would like to go to Assam.

She asked where that was and I looked up the atlas, for I wasn't all that sure myself. She said: 'Why not?'

The salary offered was seven hundred rupees a month. I looked up the exchange rate and discovered that this was approximately seven hundred pounds a year. It sounded attractive. I applied, was interviewed, and was given the job. Towards the end of 1936 we set sail.

23. 'You Just Cannae Win'

Looking back on my four years in Glasgow I see so much that might have been different, but old heads on young shoulders are far from being natural, and should not be expected.

Probably the most trying trouble in the life of a young minister is his sense of loneliness. That may seem odd for a man who has a congregation of six or seven hundred, which is far too many for a beginner. But it is a fact that at times his life is a very lonely one.

Of course, he and his wife make friends, and quite naturally they gravitate towards some more than to others. But since these usually are young couples of around their own age, they can hardly be accounted advisers or confidants, since they don't know any more about things than the couple themselves, and maybe even less.

There are older men and women who would be glad to advise and encourage, but he shrinks from unburdening himself. If isn't that he's afraid he might be rebuffed, though he may be a little afraid that he might be laughed at – or even merely smiled at. His main fear is that he won't be understood, and that the layman will not be able to appreciate that what appears to the minister to be a problem is indeed not a problem at all.

The only person who can appreciate a minister's hopes and fears and unhappiness is another minister or a doctor, maybe, if he happens to know a doctor sufficiently well.

He's a crusader, after all, this young minister. He's setting out to change the world, and if he manages to do it overnight so much the better. Of course, he does not know very much about the world, except that it ought to be changed. And he proceeds by methods best known by himself to do this thing. He discovers before very long, as most crusaders do, that it is not easy to change the world, mainly because the world has no wish to be changed but is perfectly happy the way it is.

Then there's the business of preaching. A young man in a pulpit, always nearer the ceiling than his congregation, is delivering opinions. He seldom stops to think how few these opinions are, and, bless them, neither does his congregation. They accept a great deal of very brash stuff, simply because the chap is wearing gown and bands and because they know his heart's in the right place. I think they say to themselves: 'I mind when I thought this too. He'll live and learn, the poor wee chap.'

In Glasgow I put far more work into my sermons than I do in the normal way today. There are some 'out of the run' sermons that take a great deal of work, and, of course, broadcast sermons demand everything. I wrote every word, and still do, but in the old days I underlined this line in red ink and another line in green ink according to where the emphasis ought to go. Last thing on Saturday night I read the effusion over to Margaret, one half of whom was asleep by this time while the other half was listening for the baby.

But a young man can't possibly put himself into a hundred and more sermons a year. He hasn't got enouth to put in.

For nearly thirty years, as will appear, I have been writing leading articles for the *Greenock Telegraph*, the local daily newspaper; eight hundred words a day. But there's always a subject: something in the news, national or local. But two sermons a week with no subject set! And not for three months but for forty years. I'd like some critics to try it. As I've said, the young fellow has to work harder at this than the old chap like myself. He doesn't know enough. When he comes to my age he may reckon that he knows too much. But that is no excuse for stinting his preparation. He must set out to be, and he must remain until his dying day, a craftsman at his job. And his job is to communicate what is in him to his listeners. If there is nothing in him, then obviously there is nothing to communicate, and he shouldn't be up there in the pulpit making a public demonstration of the fact.

He must school himself from the beginning to read and write; to erase and change; to scrap and to polish until he has achieved something that is as near to perfection as he, with his limitations, can accomplish. To do less is an insult to his congregation; and, just as bad, it is an insult to the God whose will he is in that pulpit to proclaim.

I have already mentioned Professor Gossip who taught us Christian Ethics and Practical Training; not, in my view, very successfully. Once he told us that, coming up the pulpit steps of his church, he met the Lord Jesus standing at the top. When he came up to him, not being able to get past, he stopped. And Jesus said to him: 'Arthur, that's a very poor thing you're giving my people today.'

I've never had that experience, though I've met the Lord Jesus several times. But I've certainly had that feeling many a time going up the pulpit steps.

'The hungry sheep look up, and are not fed.' It's a soul-destroying feeling that nobody but a minister can possibly appreciate. Unless maybe a doctor who has signed the wrong prescription.

And yet it is an odd thing: sometimes when I have felt that the sermon had got nowhere, and I was almost ashamed of having delivered it, well prepared though it always was, there has been a knock on the vestry door, and someone will come in and thank me. I may have missed the whole congregation by a long sea mile, but, for that single one, heart has spoken to heart.

On the other hand there are times when the preacher can't get through the first part of the service quickly enough. He would like to cut verses from the hymns and abbreviate the prayers, and miss out a scripture reading to get the sooner to the sermon. He's absolutely full of it; trembling with the excitement of what he has to say. He preaches his sermon, and when it's over he doesn't know how he got back to the vestry. He must have had wings. But there's no tap on the vestry door. The mood of exaltation fades and dies into the light of common day. The session clerk comes in to do something with the roll book. Somebody comes in to get their passport papers signed. The minister puts on his hat and coat and goes through to the small hall where a good many of the members foregather for a blether after service.

Nobody mentions the sermon to him, though somebody might say it was a pity he chose that closing hymn, for they didn't know it. The secretary of the choir tells him they're arranging their social and dance for a week on Friday and will he and his wife be able to come? He says that will be fine, and walks down Castle Street to the green car for home, asking himself if this is all that it is about, and his wife can't understand why he can't eat his lunch.

I must make it plain that this book is not written specially for young ministers. But it's written for what I earnestly hope is a large number of people who attend their church regularly, or even spasmodically, but who have no idea what goes on in the mind and soul of the man in the pulpit.

Maybe part of the trouble with the young minister is that he is inclined to preach *at* people. The older minister (though there are, alas, exceptions) doesn't preach *at* people. He preaches *to* people. There is a mighty difference. If now and again he feels he has to lay down the law, he makes sure in the first place that it is God's law he is laying down.

The young minister is impatient; he does not suffer fools gladly or otherwise. He is dedicated to the work of inspiring people. The wise old minister has infinite patience, and he knows that if he does not suffer fools gladly or otherwise he is going to find an awful lot of people insufferable. If he does not know this he is just an old minister. He is not yet a wise one.

He also knows that inspiration is not a commonplace, but a splendid rarity. He is not going to ring the bell every time. He is not even going to ring the bell often. He learns to be content and thankful if he rings it now and again.

I very seldom hear a sermon except on radio or television, for I don't take holidays and am very rarely out of the pulpit. But circumstances removed me from my pulpit not long ago for a month and I heard four sermons. None of them was over-long: I will admit that. Two of the men I heard obviously had a useful little book of anecdotes which they introduced at strategic points. Like the chap who is making a speech and says: 'And this reminds me of a story . . . ' He does this four times, and tries to give the impression that the whole thing has been spontaneous and that he has actually and suddenly been reminded of this story, when anybody with any experience of public speaking knows that his whole speech has been built round these four stories which he has been 'suddenly reminded' of; two of which are badly told because he takes too long over them, and the other two his audience have heard before.

Jesus, of course, introduced anecdotes: and what gems they are! Could you take away a word or add a word to one of Jesus' parables

and improve it? But these weren't really anecdotes. These were all
stored-up experience and observation.

I have written and broadcast much in humorous vein. Most of
it is from my own experience, exaggerated a little, and coloured a
little. Jerome K. Jerome, and George and Harris, undoubtedly went
up the Thames in a rowing boat. And undoubtedly things happened.
But they didn't quite happen in the way *Three Men in a Boat* says
they happened. The accolade for humour is when you tell of some
experience, and decorate it a little, and somebody says to you
afterwards: 'You know, that was awful like the thing.'

This is the wonder of the parables of Jesus, and this is why
they bit home on those who heard them: they were awful like the
thing.

But these four sermons that I heard, although, as I have said,
they were not over-long, had far too much padding in them. The meat
and the substance of the message could have been said, and said
better, in five minutes.

This has been another digression, though, let it be said, most
congregations whose offering has been taken on entering would
want some of their money back if they got only a five-minute sermon.
They would reckon that the minister wasn't properly prepared.
When, if the truth were told, the indication that the minister is
properly prepared is that his sermon is short.

The minister must never preach on bad church attendance to the
congregation of the faithful who are very seldom absent. Mind you,
I don't think I have ever done this. I chose another, and (as I thought)
more useful, time and place to do this. I never did it again. It was
in this wise.

In Scotland there is always a big turn out on communion Sunday.
Scottish churches very seldom have any more than four communion
Sundays in the year, and many have only two. I am rather in favour
of this, though I will not argue the point with those who are
not.

All the folk whom you haven't seen much of since last time
are there. They hand in their communion cards, which means that
they are marked present, and this keeps them in good standing,
even if they are not what the trade unionist would call 'fully paid
up'. I decided that this was the time and place to have words

with the backsliders, and I did. The words were not minced, either.

After the service one of the elders told me that he had been speaking to one of the more regular backsliders who had told him that my sermon had spoiled the whole communion service for him. I said that I didn't give a damn if I had spoiled the communion service for him. And I meant it.

But during the week I was visiting a dear old saintly soul who, I knew, always made excuses for me when she heard me being criticized. She said that what I had said from the pulpit on the Sunday was right enough, and that maybe it was something that had to be said. But, she said, 'The service wasn't just the same for me.' And I couldn't possibly say to myself that this was something I didn't care a damn about. It was something I cared a great deal about.

I made up my mind, then and there, that I would never do this again, no matter how great the temptation to do it. Those who take the sacrament unworthily do, according to St Paul, 'eat and drink damnation to themselves'. They need no assistance from the minister to accomplish that.

His function is to help those who care to reach the fullness of Holy Communion; they have come looking for something, and praying that they may find it. His job is, by his words, to help them. And, of course, there's no point in preaching at somebody, or at some group, who've been getting under your skin.

There was one young minister who had an officebearer who was doing just that. He was a thorn in the flesh. Later on, thorns never reach the flesh. The skin has grown too thick.

This young fellow tried everything in the way of concession and compromise, but it was no use. Nothing would penetrate. So he decided to preach a sermon on certain human characteristics and to do it so bluntly and so pointedly (if you can be blunt and pointed at the same time) that even this case-hardened character would see himself as others saw him. He preached the sermon and he put his heart and soul into it.

In the vestry he awaited the reaction, for reaction there would have to be. There was no knock on the door. This officebearer was not in the habit of knocking on vestry doors. He just opened it and walked in. The minister thought: 'Here's for it!'

'Splendid,' said the officebearer. 'Just splendid. I bet that made a lot of them sit up and take notice!'

As the man said, 'You just cannae win.'

Another subject a minister ought not to preach on is money. I did once in Glasgow and the treasurer told me I had made a mess of it. This I gladly admitted. You can't preach unless your heart's in it, and my heart wasn't in this.

This was, you will remember, during the depression, though it so happened that the more influential deacons who asked me to preach on the subject of financial responsibility were in jobs, and in reasonably good jobs. To give honour where honour is due, they accepted their responsibilities and carried a good share of the financial burden of the kirk. But in many ways I knew the congregation better than they did, for I was in and out of the homes of the 'other half', and as I was preparing the sermon it was these homes and these good people I saw in my mind's eye.

What the substance of the sermon was I can't remember, but the general conclusion was that a great many people who had very little were doing more than could be expected of them, and that if we wanted to better our financial position the others would have to do better than they were doing.

Congregational finance is not the minister's business at all, and the further he keeps away from it, the better. This is not what he is there for, and this is not what he was trained for. It is the layman's business. There may be, and indeed there are, congregations who are having a sore struggle because they have a somewhat clueless minister. But far more often the cause of the trouble is that the officebearers are not doing their job.

One minister said: 'I can get a dozen people to play the portable harmonium, but I can't get two to carry it into the street.'

As I have said, this is not a book for the young minister. There aren't enough of them to make it profitable. It's a book for the layman, who is quite certainly a decent, kindly chap, but who may not appreciate the difficulties of a job which is vastly different from any other job on earth.

There have been a lot of 'don'ts' in the last few pages, and since nobody has any right to say 'don't' unless he has done the daft thing himself, it should be clear that all this advice comes out of experience. Another 'don't' for the young minister is this: don't introduce your own ideas when your officebearers don't like to be told, or even to have it implied, that what they have been doing for years could possibly (or even easily) be done better.

The wise minister 'sells' his ideas one at a time, and never to more than two officebearers at a time, privately and almost casually. He just throws out the idea in the passing, as a sower sows the seed, and hopes that it has fallen into the good ground.

The chaps he has spoken to go away and meditate. They discuss the thing with other chaps, never mentioning where the original idea came from, of course. By this time it has become their own idea. They mention it to their wife, and since she knows a lot more about the church and its moods and prejudices than he does, she gives her opinion with some force and at considerable length.

Eventually the idea is broached at a meeting. The minister sits back and listens, occasionally saying a word or two to indicate that he thinks there might be something in it. And in no time at all the deed is done.

So, friend, if your minister takes you aside and mentions something in an offhand kind of way, you will now know what he is after. When the thing is accomplished, there is no harm in telling him so.

As far as conduct of the service is concerned, however, the minister is on his own, and he must remain on his own. This is his privilege, and it is his obligation. At the same time there are ways and ways of making changes. You don't make changes just for the sake of making changes, and we must not forget that what is established and accepted has stood the test of time.

Four or five singings, two prayers, two scripture readings, a children's address, a sermon, the offering: these have been part and parcel of the Scottish service for generations. There are those who would like to change this order, but before they begin they ought to ask themselves why this way of doing things should have been established and accepted for so long. There is no point or purpose in change for the sake of change.

Of course, in the Scottish way there was very little 'audience participation'. There were no responses or the like. Everything that was said was said by the man in the pulpit. But this is easily remedied.

The Lord's Prayer should be spoken by the whole congregation, and why not read the Old Testament lesson antiphonally? That is, one verse from the pulpit, the next verse read by the whole congregation. I have done this for years, and people like it. For one thing it makes them turn up their Bibles.

Of course, there are dangers in the practice, for there are books of the Bible that are not all that easy to find, and it's reckoned cheating to look up the index. The volume from the congregation varies in a calculable ratio to the obscurity of the Book selected. As Hendry said in *A Window in Thrums*: 'Anybody can turn up the Psalms of David but it takes an able-bodied man to find Zechariah.'

A general conclusion to these rambling remarks might be that there is something to be said for bishops. Young ministers need not only advice and guidance; they need control and discipline. In fact I think I might thoroughly approve of bishops in the Church of Scotland if they made me one of them.

I did another silly thing before leaving Barony North. This book might well be sub-titled *Those foolish things*. An acquaintance who was editor of a weekly newspaper invited me to write an article on why I was leaving Glasgow for Assam. It could have been a very short article, for the main reason was economic and financial. But there were other reasons, some of which I have touched on earlier. There was the multiplicity of churches in the centre of the town, duplication of work and the resulting financial strain on resources. I wrote about this, but was careful to preface the article with an assurance that I was not referring specifically to Barony North, a congregation which was second to none.

I sent in the article and the editor phoned and said it was just a little too long, and would I mind if he edited it slightly. Being then unlearned in the ways of the press, I said I did not mind in the least. He edited out the preface. I don't say I left Barony North under a cloud, but the climate could have been sunnier.

24. A Chaplain in Assam

We sailed from Tilbury on the BI ship *Mulbera* with Captain Grant Pyves. We had sold most of the furniture, paid our debts and were left with a little – a very little. There's a tremendous difference in the price of furniture when you're selling it not buying it.

The voyage was not really eventful for the three of us: daughter Margaret being just two and a half at the time, an age when everything is either eventful or commonplace.

Not knowing the drill, I was unaware of the fact that if you want a good place at the dining-room tables you have to square the chief steward. The other stewards were Goanese. Because of this omission we found ourselves placed far below the salt, beside a sergeant of the Scots Greys and his wife who were going to an Eastern posting and an ex-jockey who was taking some horses out to race in Colombo. They were nice folk and we got on famously.

A general meeting of the passengers was called after we were through the Bay of Biscay. They had to make sure of a quorum. Daughter and I were fine, and did full justice to the menu, and Margaret was the same, having had some practice on the *Glen Rosa* and *Atalanta*.

The general meeting of passengers was to arrange the various committees which would make our stay on board so pleasant, and which were a pain in the neck. Every time you were getting on with your book, or quietly dozing off, someone would slap you on the back and tell you that you were due to play in the fourth round of the shuffle board.

They must have discovered from the passenger list that I had a university degree, and so could almost certainly read and write. They appointed me secretary. This threw me a great deal into the company of the chief steward, helping him to edit the daily duplicated news-sheet. He suggested that he could manage to get us accommodation nearer the captain's table. Like the humble man in the parable we were being asked to move up higher. I indicated that we were perfectly happy where we were.

At Calcutta the chief steward stood at the head of the gangway to bid farewell to the passengers and to accept such tangible recognition as they cared to offer for his efforts on their behalf during the voyage. As we passed him by, I bade him farewell.

We stayed for a day or two in Calcutta, had lunch in the Bengal Club, which was very exclusive, and attended service in St Andrew's Church. Scotsmen always become very religiously inclined when they go abroad and discover a St Andrew's Church. And there are not very many places they can go to without discovering one.

Then the train on the Dacca line, transfer to the river steamer on the Brahmaputra, train again on the other side and so to South Sylhet which is to the east of what is now Bangladesh. The padre bungalow was on the Jagcherra Tea Estate. There were three rooms, each with a concrete floor. Each ran the width of the house, the peak of the roof, in the middle, being precariously supported by a perpendicular girder which had been badly twisted in the Bihar earthquake.

There was one bathroom. The bungalow stood on a low hill, which meant that the water had to be pumped up from a well at the foot of the hill, to a tank which afforded a gravity supply. The hot water was delivered from the cookhouse in five-gallon kerosene tins.

Margaret had been warned early not to investigate the cookhouse or the servants' quarters, which were congregated behind the bungalow. But you know what women are.

Fish were conveyed home from the bazaar in the same kerosene tins, and were left to swim out the remainder of their days in a concrete tank in the cookhouse. One day Margaret tempted providence and went to investigate, discovering that the fish were back in the tins, and the cook was in the fishpool, soaping himself generously to the accompaniment of a bawdy Bengali ballad.

There was no road up the hill to the bungalow. The car, supplied by the Indian Tea Association, had to be left at the bottom, and the rest of the journey home had to be completed up a long flight of steps cut out of the hillside. In the rains these were mud.

If I had thought (which, I am ashamed to confess, I did think) that I might manage to save some money out of the fabulous stipend of seven hundred rupees a month, I was soon to think again. To begin with, there were the servants. The normal staff for a bungalow was one bearer, or butler; one *khansamah*, or cook; two *malis*, or gardeners; two *chowkedars,* or general dogsbodies; and one sweeper.

The hardest work the day *chowkedar* did was to waken up the night *chowkedar* before he went off duty, and to show his appreciation, the night *chowkedar* would do the same for him twelve hours later. For this useful service they each got ten rupees a month. It doesn't sound a lot, but it was amazing what a rupee would buy, if you had humble tastes, and plenty of time to haggle with the supplier in the bazaar. The *malis* got ten a month too, though their main job was not gardening, but pumping the water up to the tank.

It was necessary, too, to have a car boy, for if you were going anywhere and got a flat tyre, you were so soaked with sweat by the time you got the wheel changed that you just were not presentable. He got fifteen a month, being a member of the domestic aristocracy.

If you had a horse (and I was not long in acquiring one, as will duly appear) this set you back twenty rupees, and there had to be a grass *wallah* who collected fodder by weeding the tea. Having a daughter, there had to be an *ayah*, a Khasia woman who rated twenty-five a month. The wage bill for this little lot was around a hundred and sixty-five rupees a month, which made a considerable hole in the seven hundred. I was also sending money home to Mother (I forgot if it was a hundred or a hundred and fifty rupees a month, but it certainly wasn't less).

It was immediately obvious that all these servants were not needed, but we were up against trade unionism, Eastern version. Apart from bearer and cook, and *ayah* if necessary, a planter had his other servants paid for by the garden. When I called a servants' meeting and suggested that some of them might be better employed doing an honest day's work with the tea instead of getting in one another's road in the bungalow, they pointed out that this was the staff carried by the planters' bungalows and that it had to be the staff carried by the padre bungalow. This was a regulation introduced, apparently, by the Medes and Persians at some time in the past.

Sylhet is an extension of the Bengal plains and is as flat as a pancake, crossed by low ridges which hardly qualify as hills, and which divide the territory into so-called valleys where the tea is grown. The largest of these valleys was Balisera, where our home was to be for some years. There were roads of sorts leading to other valleys passable in the dry season, but during the rains tending from the difficult to the impossible.

The tea produced in South Sylhet was not vintage stuff like the tea of Darjeeling, but it was strong liquoring and formed the basis of many blends. The planters never thought they got enough for it on the Calcutta market.

To the north was Cachar and beyond that was Manipur and the border of Burma. Farther to the north were the high hills which split Assam into two, and up on top was the capital, Shillong, reached by a rather hair-raising road. These were the Khasia, Jaintia, and Naga hills.

Shillong was the hot weather resort for those who could afford it, and was the centre of a Welsh Mission which supported the only hospital in the territory, founded, built, and equipped by a brilliant surgeon by the name of Roberts. Here the planters' babies were born at considerable expense.

There was a very small branch of the Welsh Mission on Jagcherra garden, but the missionaries did not visit it very often, leaving most of the work to be done by a Christian *babu* (a *babu* is an English-speaking Bengali) who came from Maulvi Bazaar on Sundays.

On one occasion I married a couple in the wee bamboo church. I hadn't been out long and my Hindustani was still a bit sketchy and certainly not up to the demands of a marriage service. I got hold of the doctor *babu* who looked after the garden hospital, and got him to translate the marriage service from the Book of Common Order into phonetic Hindustani. As far as most of the words were concerned, it might have been the funeral service that I read. But the couple took hands and made their vows and I pronounced them man and wife. I managed that without the book.

Garden Hindustani, or *bhat*, was a very simple lingua franca, if Hindustani can be a lingua franca. The Indians spoke it with a Scots accent. People don't believe this, but it's perfectly true. The gardens were opened up originally by Scottish firms, notably, Finlay's,

Duncan's and Buchanan's among others. They had to get labour, and a great deal of labour.

The Assamese peasant wasn't interested. He had his own croft which he cultivated, and though he might take a seasonal job at jungle-clearing or the like, he didn't want a round-the-year job. Labour had to be brought in from the United Provinces, the Central Provinces, Santalia and elsewhere, and all these folk spoke their own language, or vastly different variants of the same language.

They learned a new language from the planters: a form of Hindustani spoken with a Scots accent. The result was that although the syntax of my infantile efforts at the tongue left much to be desired my accent was flawless. Not like daughter Margaret's.

We hadn't been there very long, and were entertaining some of the bachelor planters one Sunday. Young Margaret was playing on the carpet, probably picking fleas off the dog. I called the *chowkedar* to give him some instruction, and could not quite find the appropriate words. The planters refused to help. The *chowkedar's* face showed no sign of dawning understanding. This was partly his fault, for he was not the brightest of souls. But it was more my fault.

One of the planters said at length: 'Get Margaret to tell him, padre.' I appealed to the innocent child, and without looking up she said something out of the corner of her mouth and the *chowkedar* departed like a scalded cat.

I asked the planters to explain. It transpired that she had given him a brief sketch of his antecedents before telling him what to do. Which he did with alacrity. Perfect praise may come out of the mouths of babes and sucklings. This, apparently, was not in that category.

Of course she spent a great deal of her time with the servants, and vastly preferred the curries which Abdul the bearer made for himself to those which the cook served up to us. Before she left for home at the age of five her Hindustani was fluent, and she had more than a smattering of Bengali, Santali, and Khasi. By the time she reached home she had forgotten the lot.

The river Surma flows through Sylhet to join the Brahmaputra, which in turn joins the Ganges, and our cavalry regiment of the Auxiliary Force of India was the Surma Valley Light Horse, which every male who was hale and hearty joined while he was hale and hearty. So did I.

Cachar had A squadron, Sylhet had B squadron, and great was the rivalry between the two. B squadron was divided into B Left and B Right. Balisera, with Luskerpore, formed B Left, and we regarded ourselves as the crack troop. As a matter of fact, we were.

The government provided the uniform and the weaponry. You had to provide your own horse for whose upkeep His Majesty, or the Viceroy, or somebody with money, gave you forty rupees a month for food, attention, upkeep, and spare parts. A regular sergeant major was attached to the troop. He measured me for my uniform.

This does not mean that the uniform was tailor-made. He just looked at me once and decided from which of three shelves he would take the garments: normal, extra big, or small. These uniforms were war-surplus material. Some of them were reputed to have been worn by Allenby's troops when they rode through the gates of Jerusalem. I had a strong suspicion that they had been worn by Kitchener's troops in South Africa.

There was a khaki tunic for church parades which were held once a year at camp. You had to supply your own shirt. In addition there were riding breeches, puttees, and ammunition boots with spurs.

The topi was an enormous thing like a massive candle extinguisher and you wore a leather bandolier with your ammunition. When you lay down at the butts to shoot, the bandolier came up under the brim of the topi at the back and knocked the front down over your eyes. This made aiming rather difficult. The thing to do was to pull out the leather sweat band, and insert your skull into this. It might have been frowned on at Sandhurst, but probably would have passed at Bisley. I discovered, rather to my surprise, that I was a good shot.

I am right-handed, but the only eye I can see very much with is my left one, which means that I have to shoot off the left shoulder. For rapid fire this is more an asset than it is a liability, for when you get the rifle firmly embedded in the sandbag, and hold the butt firmly into the shoulder with the left hand, finger on trigger, you can work the bolt with the right hand and make the thing go like a machine gun. I could always get my fifteen off in a minute, and twenty, with ten in the magazine for a start. But I didn't have a horse.

I let it be known that the padre was in the market for a horse, and one day a native from a neighbouring valley appeared leading an animal which had all the external appearance of the noble steed. He also bore a letter which indicated that the upset price, including saddlery, was one hundred rupees (seven pounds ten).

This should have made me suspicious, but I do not have a suspicious mind. And, after all, the cook could buy a young goat in the bazaar for five annas. By the time it reached the table it was mutton. The owner, it seemed, was going on leave. He wanted the faithful animal to have a good home. The fact was that he was abandoning it, but I was not to learn this until later. I paid the money, and gave orders that the animal was to be fed, watered, and produced in the morning properly dressed.

Next morning they led it round and parked it at the side of the verandah, which was very convenient for mounting horses. I mounted. The horse stood up on its hind legs and I slid over its tail. I remounted. The Dows are made of stern stuff, which is appropriate enough, for over the stern went Dow again. Undeterred, I clambered on board once more.

The horse looked round in surprise, or possibly in respect. It went through the same motions, but this time Dow was prepared. With my right hand I clung to the cantle of the saddle as the cowboys do when they think nobody's looking. The horse resignedly went through the motions once more. Dow sat firm, and a horse cannot stand on its hind legs forever without getting signed on by a circus. It came down, but not, I later gathered, because mind had triumphed over matter. It just wanted a rest, and time for meditation. Then it uprose once more.

By this time I was feeling confident. The brute could go on like this all day if it liked. Dow would outlast it. Unfortunately this animal, although it had a splendid chest, tended to tail off towards the waist. On a smaller scale he would have made a very shapely greyhound. The girth began to slip. The grip on the cantle was of no avail. It simply meant that this time when I went over the tail I was accompanied by the saddle.

With a faint but most objectionable smile, the horse stepped out of the girth, which by this time was round his hind feet, just as a man might step out of his pyjamas before taking a bath. He then returned to the stable to see if there was anything to eat.

I got the car out and went to see Rab, the local expert in equine matters. He asked me where I'd got the horse. I told him. He said that this was an animal which was regularly sold to every new assistant who came out to tea. He told me it was a rearer.

I informed him that I was well aware of this, since I had been contemplating its rear for half the morning. I asked if there was anything that could be done about a rearer, short of shooting it. He said he didn't think so, but he had heard or read somewhere, though he had never seen the thing actually demonstrated, that if the rider equipped himself with a club, and hit the brute between the ears whenever its head came up, it might be persuaded to keep its feet on the ground. He gave no guarantee that it would work.

But I remembered the story in Kipling's *Soldiers Three* which tells how Mulvaney tamed the elephant with the butt of his rifle. I repaired back to the bungalow and gave instruction for the preparation of a suitably offensive weapon against the morrow.

No doubt when he was saddled next morning, the horse sighed and said to himself: 'Here we go again.' If so, he was wrong. The moment the ears went back and the head started to come up, he bought it plumb on the sconce and his forelegs hit the ground with a jarring thud.

As Goliath of Gath might have said when the stone from David's sling impinged upon his brow, such a thing had never entered his head before.

I will say to the credit of that horse, though, that he was no quitter. He tried it again three times, each time with the same result. He would have shaken his head in bewilderment, but it was too painful. I kicked him in the ribs and we moved off placidly. I kept swinging the club within his line of vision just to let him see that Dow was ware and waking. The message was received. Then in the distance I saw the manager's wife approaching on her milk-white steed. Something would have to be done, and quickly.

The well-appointed rider may carry in his hand a quirt: he may swing a polo stick for practice. But a club which would not have been out of place holding up a snooker table was something entirely different. For the last time I swung it forward and gave the beast a minatory tap on the skull, then dropped the weapon surreptitiously into the tea just as the lady came round the corner.

Whereupon the horse stood on up its hind legs and I slid gracelessly over its tail. There is nothing in the manual of etiquette which tells you how to raise your hat when sitting in the middle of a road looking at a horse's tail. The horse looked rather pleased. Possibly he thought I was raising my hat to him.

Shortly afterwards I gave him away. A young chap had just come out to a neighbouring valley. I hadn't the heart to sell it to him. I retained the saddlery in the hope that another horse might come along whom the dress fitted. But there were always chaps going home on leave who wanted a horse looked after. I was never without at least one. And later I got a new one from Australia.

I was never a very good horseman, being a little short in the leg, but I will say that when playing polo I came off rather more seldom than some others in a more exalted station in life. It is the greatest game in life, being beaten only by the game of life itself.

But this was not work, although through it, and especially through the regiment, I got to know and respect the chaps, and they got to know, and (I hope) respect me. At the start, however, I got a bucket of cold water thrown over my enthusiasm.

In the Balisera valley there was a church of sorts, of clay and wattles made, and a wire cage over the piano to keep the rats out. In half a dozen other valleys the services were held in the clubs after the Sunday-afternoon tennis. The men wore ties for service and the women wore hats and carried their handbags.

I had no idea what the religious convictions of the planters were, far less of their denominational affinities. But after a few months I thought we should have in each valley a communion service. But I certainly was not going to confine this to Church of Scotland members.

I started with Balisera and sent out a circular to each bungalow announcing the service on a certain date, and saying that since there was no communion roll I invited everyone. All who came would be the future communicant membership. There was a very big response.

The service was in the old Scots style with the people sitting down the sides, while in the middle and stretching the length of the church was a long white-spread table. At the appropriate time, and singing the communion hymn, the folk moved over and took up their places at the table. The bread was native baked, the wine was in a cup won at a race meeting. It was a very simple service as a communion service ought to be, and it was very moving, for these people were thinking of home, and of parents and children they had not seen for a while.

Somebody (and I learned later who it was) sent a copy of the circular to the Presbytery in Calcutta. I won't say I got a rocket; call it just rather a stiff letter, informing me that this was not the way to do things at all, but that the names of all wishing to become communicant members should have been sent to the Kirk Session of St Andrew's, Calcutta, along with disjunction certificates or evidence of instruction in a class for first communicants. That was the first and last communion service.

There wasn't very much call for what might be called the routine work of the ministry. Serious illness was dealt with in Calcutta. Planters either married when they were home on leave or the girl came out and they were married in Calcutta. There were not many baptisms. Planters couldn't afford large families.

I conducted only one marriage. The groom wasn't a planter but an engineer with the river steamers on the Ganges, but the resident engineer at Fenchuganj on the Surma asked me if I would oblige. The wedding was during the rains, and we had to abandon the car and cross the rice fields by country boat. It was quite an affair. The Indian staff, who love celebration and pageant, had erected a magnificent bamboo archway bearing the words: 'God save the bride'.

In one bachelor bungalow there was the photograph of a lassie I used to court in school. In another was a Sunday School prize signed by my father, and almost every Scotsman knows another Scotsman who happens to know some other Scotsman.

Life out there could be splendid; it could also be rather mean and petty. It was a man's world: women didn't have enough to do, though that wasn't their fault. And in those days, although the manager's bungalow could be palatial, very often the assistants' bungalows were anything but.

I got into a bit of trouble with one of the companies for writing an article for a home magazine on the conditions their assistants had to live in. Though I will say the article did some good and there was an improvement.

You see, viewed through the eyes of a young Scots lassie who has fallen for this sun-tanned young planter home on leave, the dream of life on the gardens is glamorous indeed: the club, afternoon tea parties, tennis, golf, the gathering for polo on a Sunday, and all these servants! Just sit back and clap your hands and a bottle of champagne comes falling out of a cupboard. The reality was far different then. I don't know what it's like now.

The bungalow was of course furnished. This means that the bedroom has two iron beds in it with a mosquito net over them which means that you're sleeping in a kind of marquee. There is also a kind of wardrobe called an *almirah*. On the concrete floor is a *moonj* mat made by those who are languishing in jail. The dining-room furniture if offered to a respectable Women's Guild for their annual jumble sale would be refused indignantly.

Her husband's pay is four hundred rupees a month, off which he is trying to run a car which has already changed hands four times, as owners going home on leave tried to raise some cash. Her nearest neighbour could be five miles away or even twenty miles away. Her man has his work to do, and since she doesn't know the language she's got nobody to talk to. Then there is protocol. Everything goes by seniority, and since she's been last to arrive, she's tail-end Tilly till another innocent arrives.

Things will certainly be vastly different now, but in my day an assistant came out on three hundred rupees a month for his first five years. He then went on leave and his pay went up to four hundred, where it remained until he got an acting management to allow some manager to get his leave. The assistant then advanced to five hundred and stayed there until he became a manager in his own right.

These appointments came on strict seniority, which meant that if two men came out on the same boat, and one had to travel further than the other to reach the garden he was assigned to, the chap with the shorter journey was senior to him for the rest of their life in tea. The men did not like this much; the wives hated it. Or at least the wife of the junior man hated it. Sometimes she made no bones about saying so.

The addition to the salary was commission on the profits of the garden, which was all right if the garden was showing any profit. But the commission, too, depended on seniority.

Then there was the business of the family. If a baby came along, it was a case of Calcutta or Shillong, though there were able doctors in the valleys. When it came to leave at the specified time, the firm paid the wife's passage home. If she wanted to go home earlier, the planter paid it himself. When the child was around five, he or she had to be taken or sent home to school. And the planter had to pay for that too. Now, I believe, families are flown out for the school holidays and flown back again at the firm's expense.

As a result of all this many of the assistants – indeed, a majority, I would surmise – remained bachelors. Which was not always a good thing.

Contrary to general supposition the planters were not the sons of the aristocracy. Not even the younger sons whom Kipling wrote about. It was time-served engineers the firms usually looked for.

During the plucking season the whole garden had to be covered once a week; otherwise the leaves become too tough. A breakdown in the factory machinery was therefore a very serious business. In the dry, or non-plucking, season the factory machinery, from the prime mover down to the pulleys, had to be overhauled and repaired, this required a skilled engineer. The assistants also had to build the bridges, maintain the roads, dig the wells and build the sheds, usually with the help of a Chinaman who was always called John.

Shooting was good; duck, pheasant, pigeon, and especially the *jungli moorghi*, who is the ancestor of the farmyard fowl and is the wiliest of birds, always feeding in the middle of an open expanse of *dhan khett*, or rice field, after the grain has been cut, and where there is no cover at all. If you can crawl near enough to them you're well entitled to shoot a sitting bird. When I shot, I shot for the pot, for they were the best of eating. Except occasionally when

some of the natives would come to complain that the deer or the
wild pigs were destroying their rice.

There's nothing snobbish in calling them 'natives', of course.
Everyone is a native of his own country.

But this was night shooting, with an electric bulb worn on an
elastic band round the forehead, and switched on when you heard
the animal chewing. Twice I sat up for tiger without getting a shot.
We saw them occasionally, and once we got a leopard in the head-
lights on a jungle road. It behaved just like a rabbit and couldn't
get out of the light until we came to a corner.

When we went out to India I was terrified of snakes, though the
only one I had ever seen was a grass snake at home. In five years
I saw perhaps a dozen all told, and only one in the bungalow,
though that was a young cobra which I despatched with a polo
stick.

I never heard of any of the garden workers being bitten by a
snake, though they were working in the tea where the bushes are
so close together that you can't see the ground. One planter who
had been out for thirty years told me that he had never known of a
case of snake bite either. His theory of the snake-bite fatalities of
Indian statistics was that a large number of people wanted to get
rid of other people and blamed the snakes.

There were plenty of python in the jungle, but snakes are nervous
creatures, though inclined to be a trifle deaf. Jungle travellers are
safe enough if they make enough noise; and your Indian makes
plenty of that.

Whatever may have been said by those who miscall the old
British Raj just because it was the British Raj, it was not true in
my day of the tea gardens. The pay was more than adequate, and
was mostly on a piece-work basis. There was work for the whole
family and it wasn't very heavy work. They were well housed and
sanitation was good, even if it was not always used. There was a
school of sorts and a properly equipped hospital supervised by the
doctor *babu* and visited at least once a week, and daily in emergency,
by the British doctor employed by the company.

Maternity benefit was paid, the woman ceasing work a couple
of months before the baby was due, and again after having the baby.
A bonus was paid if the baby was alive and kicking after a year.

There were plenty of babies, and mortality among them was very small. This wasn't all done out of the goodness of the firm's heart, of course. Tea can't be plucked mechanically, though I believe the Japs tried it. An adequate and contented labour force is essential. The British-owned gardens had it; Indian-owned gardens were rather different.

While we were there the Congress troubles were on, though their activity was mainly in the towns. Occasionally an agitator would appear, and in one or two rare spots managed to create some trouble. But not often. The average man or woman working on a British tea garden didn't know what the agitator was talking about, and couldn't have cared less.

Changes were taking place, however, and not always for the better. Summary justice had been meted out by the manager and most managers were trusted and respected, and they all knew all the circumstances of any alleged crime. But this was now frowned on by the authorities, with the result that the law courts became busier, and the pleaders, or native 'lawyers' became more and more prosperous. The managers not only knew where to look for trouble, but when to look for it, and when to turn a blind eye.

Money-lending was a curse, and the main cause of debt was the marriage of a daughter, the groom insisting it be made worth his while to take the daughter off Father's hands. The garden was usually prepared to make an adequate advance, calculated on the known ability of the family to pay it back over a period. But money-lenders are plausible characters who play on the human tendency not only to keep up with the Joneses, but to get ahead of them. A swell wedding is something not confined to the master race, though morning coats were not normally worn on the gardens. They aren't normally worn in Britain either, except at weddings and Ascot.

One night in the club, where we foregathered three nights a week or so, I asked some of the chaps if the Indians had some kind of traditional sport, which we could organize and encourage among the thousands employed on the gardens. The answers I got were not satisfactory. It appeared that the only national sports would be better discouraged, and certainly did not require any organization by us.

I suggested that we should form an inter-garden football league. The firms thought it a good idea and put up a trophy and gave permission to managers to use garden money for grounds and equipment. We made out the rules, one of which was that only one sahib could play for each garden team. I was responsible for this rule, since Jagcherra had only one assistant (who didn't play football), while other gardens had three or four. I was also aware that I was probably the best European player in the valley. This is not being immodest, for some time later, when one of the big gardens challenged an 'outside' team, I was the only white man whom they asked to play for them. We got beaten.

So, on Jagcherra garden we went down to the recently constructed football pitch, which at one time seemed to have been a Mohammedan cemetery. We were always kicking up pieces of bone. There had to be instruction, for these lads were starting off at the point a Scots boy has already reached before he goes to school. In other words, when the ball was kicked off nineteen players gathered round it and tried to hack it in the general direction of the opponents' goal. The reason why only nineteen of them did this is that the goal-keepers had been forbidden to leave their goals. I was the other one.

The first training session was like a break-in at Parkhead. Or like a break-in at Ibrox. Far be it from me to be sectarian.

Of course, they played in their bare feet. I played in rubber-soled, canvas-sided snipe boots. If you think that this gave me any advantage you are completely mistaken, never having felt the hardness of the Indian bare foot. The one to be sorry for is the one who gets in the road, and who is likely to get a big-toe nail embedded in some part of his anatomy.

But after some weeks the Jagcherra team began to emerge as something to be reckoned with, and this was by no means on my account. Though indirectly it was. I discovered that my car boy had the makings of a goalkeeper. What he did not have the makings of – or even the leavings of – was a car boy. But I had to retain him on my staff in case any of the *babus* read him the sports page of a British newspaper and he asked for a transfer to one of the bigger gardens where they could offer more money.

We played in the black and white stripes favoured by St Mirren, who is the patron saint of Paisley and who, as far as I know, never played football in his life.

There was also an annual rugby match between Sylhet and Cachar in which everything short of deliberate mayhem was committed without the interference of the police or benefit of clergy. The police were not present and I was personally involved.

25. Outpost of Empire

Although malaria didn't trouble me Margaret got it rather badly, so in June 1939 we decided that she would be better at home. At the same time daughter Margaret was about due for school. They went to live in Largs, and, of course, in September war was declared. We all volunteered.

Every member of the SVLH was on the reserve of officers for the Indian Army, and naturally the whole thing broke down. There would have been nobody to produce tea, and how on earth can you conduct a satisfactory war without tea? Some of the younger planters, however, got permission to apply, and since I wasn't a planter I took it on myself to apply without permission. Another chap and myself went up to Sylhet town to be examined by the Civil Surgeon, Colonel Daboo.

In the morning we were given some tests including one which shall be nameless, and which need not be named to anyone who has gone up for an army medical. Neither of us could produce the evidence required. We were instructed to go and have lunch, and to return later.

We went to a neighbouring planter's bungalow for lunch, which was curry, cold lager being supplied to cool us off. After that we were quite sure of success at the second attempt, but nature had other ideas, and before we left the bungalow the sample had literally gone down the drain.

Meanwhile, back at the surgery, the colonel was waiting for us, and handed us two phials. By combining our resources we managed a sufficiency, though, looking back, I appreciate that if one of us had been diabetic we both were, according to the evidence. I was turned down for bad eyesight. I produced printed proof of my ability with a rifle. On the nominal roll of the SVLH I was classed as a marksman. The colonel pointed out in a kindly way to me that if anything happened to my left eye, it wasn't a rifle but a white stick for me. The other chap was turned down too, but it had nothing to do with me.

Finance, or the lack of it, was becoming an increasing problem. Apart from other commitments, Margaret and the offspring had to be maintained at home. The obvious economy was the servants. What did I need with this troop of retainers doing practically nothing but fall into a line on pay day? Abdul the bearer and I held a committee meeting.

He was a great chap, Abdul: thoroughly reliable and absolutely trustworthy. He and I went into conference. The staff had to be cut. To do this, of course, was not adding to the total of unemployed in the garden. It was rather reducing it. On the garden there was plenty of work. In the bungalow half of them were unemployed, though they were getting paid.

Abdul said that he could combine the offices of bearer and cook. He did not suggest any extra money, but in appreciation I offered him five rupees, which he accepted. The cook wasn't much good anyway. He went on periodic benders, though as a Muslim strong drink was forbidden him. I don't know how much drink is consumed in Mohammedan countries, but by the evidence of my experience it must be considerable. I suppose there are Jews who take ham with their eggs.

After these benders the cook would send Abdul for me and I would go to the cook's house, and find him lying in a state which indicated that the undertaker could be called any minute.

'*Howah band hai, sahib,*' he would groan, which being interpreted meaneth that respiration was difficult and would shortly cease.

I gave him a good testimonial, however, for he did make a good mulligatawny soup.

Next on the list was the sweeper, who had practically nothing to do, since we lived in the post-thunder-box age of reasonable sanitation. If there was a dog he occupied himself in the time-consuming and relaxing occupation of removing fleas and depositing them in a tin of Jeyes fluid. This allowed time for ample meditation. But by this time I did not have a dog and was perfectly capable of doing all the meditation required by the establishment.

F

The *jari-wallah,* or sweeper, is, of course, an outcast. This does not mean that he once had a caste but was expelled for not paying his dues. It simply means that he and his forbears never had a caste, and had found that there is no way of getting into one.

God created the Brahman from his mouth; the Kashattriya from his arms; the Vaishiya from his thighs; and the Shudra from his feet. You are either one of these or you are nothing. And India will never get anywhere until they get rid of this.

A lot of nonsense is talked about the caste man throwing away his food if the shadow of the outcast falls across it. I never saw a caste man refusing anything if he thought nobody was watching him. Just like old Mrs McDade with her mince on a Friday.

Gandhi, of course, deliberately made himself outcast, and the people worshipped him. So it was exit *jari-wallah* to do some honest work on the garden.

We called in one of the *chowkedars* who rejoiced in the name of Joseph. He was, within the meaning of the act, a Christian. I have never understood why missionaries, when they baptize a convert to Christianity, give him a Jewish name. He was neither bright nor energetic, which of course had nothing to do with the fact that he was a Christian. There are millions of Christians who are neither bright nor energetic. Abdul and I explained the situation to him. Would Joseph take on the sweeping and the dusting in addition to his other duties which hardly took him five minutes anyway? Joseph refused.

He explained to the best of his ability that as a Christian he had a certain amount of respect from his fellows. Doing the work of a *jari-wallah,* he would have none. A theological debate then ensued in which Abdul insisted that he, a practising Mohammedan, would have no compunction in doing a *jari-wallah's* job, and would think nothing of tidying up the bathroom. He remarked that the padre sahib would have no hesitation in doing the same.

Joseph still refused. I offered him more money, though I will admit this was a little unfair. But full marks to Joseph. He stuck to his principles. Either that or he had a rooted aversion to work. I told him he would have to do more of that since I was going to employ only one *chowkedar* instead of two, and he departed for the back premises to resume his interrupted slumbers.

One of the *malis* followed suit, though I had to retain the car boy (the chap who was the good goal-keeper) and the *sais* whose care was the horses.

Life went on as usual, with me going on tour more on horseback than I had done when Margaret was with me. There were the funerals of a couple of men I hadn't known existed. They were planters who had gone native. One of them died of cholera in a village at the back of beyond. We collected the body, swimming in disinfectant, and buried him in the little cemetery.

The other fellow hadn't quite lost the place. After being sacked from the garden where he had been an assistant years before he had refused the firm's offer to send him home, and had obtained the management of a small Indian-owned garden far in the jungle. He settled down with an Indian woman who bore him a son. I knew nothing about this till word came that he was dead. And in India, for reasons that don't have to be gone into, burial must follow death rather swiftly. This was some months before Margaret went home. I got rough directions on how to find this garden and eventually found it. Some had said there was a road, some had said there was not from our side, so I went on my stout horse, Appin.

There was a boy about five years old, his mother, and an old grandmother. She could have been forty-five, she could have been ninety. And she was the problem. The Indian police were there too, and, at the risk of causing an international incident, my impression was that they were there to see if there was anything worth lifting. There wasn't very much.

I made a rough inventory of the contents of the house, which was more a glorified shack than it was a bungalow, and told the police that arrangements would have to be made for the sale of the effects for the sake of the boy. I had heard rumours that he had Anglo-Indian relatives in Calcutta, who still had to be traced.

The Anglo-Indian, for whom I always felt heartily sorry, has never been better described than by John Masters in *Bhowani Junction*. They ran the railways and they ran the postal service, and they lived in mortal terror of the day when India would acquire independence and they would be out on their ear. If Britain does not have an awful sin to answer for, then a large number of Britons have.

The boy, by the name of Sandy, wore a blue blazer, shorts, a shirt, and the inevitable topi. By this time many of us weren't wearing topis (that is, the sun helmet) because we had discovered that this business of mad dogs and Englishmen going out in the midday sun without an enormous pith helmet was just a legend. But your Anglo-Indian would not give up his topi for love nor money, and he got very little of either. Wearing a topi kept him British. Wee Sandy wore a topi.

Having ridden over the road, I told the mother that I would be back next day with the car. I thought I could make it. I did. Sandy was there, complete with blazer and topi; so was his mother, with all her goods and chattels. And so was Grannie who was determined not to be left behind.

I went through the man's papers in the hope of finding some clues to various matters. There weren't just stacks of them; there were heaps of them all over the floors.

There is not, as far as I know, an Olympic award for a standing back jump from a crouching position. Had there been I would have had a gold (had any judges been present), and would have got my name into *The Guinness Book of Records*.

Rummaging through a pile of papers, I put my hand on a karait. In case the reader does not know what a karait is, I had better explain that he is a small snake with a venom compared with which a cobra's contribution is something you might order in a milk bar. Fortunately, I think, he must have been asleep at the moment of impact. Thereafter I rather lost interest in the archives.

In the afternoon the sale of goods took place. The police were present. There wasn't much to sell: an odd piece of Indian silver, some reasonably good Benares brass, and a cage of mynas, who, as talking birds, are far ahead of parrots. The police lolled in chairs, smoking with insolent and almost aggressive indifference, which was their way of telling me that the days of the British Raj in the land were numbered. I did my best with the bidding, trying to push up the price. One of the better types told me afterwards that I had been wasting my time. They had already fixed the prices. I got nothing.

There were debts to be paid, which the Indian Tea Association attended to. I brought back Sandy, his mother and Grannie, and

didn't know what to do with them. Fortunately a very good friend
of mine and his wife, John and Jean Purvis of the Baraoora garden,
said that they would fix them up for a night or two. We were frightened that the mother might remove the blazer and the topi and
disappear with Sandy.

I mentioned the matter to the Jagcherra manager, Tom Arthur,
and he undertook to build a house for them at the back of our
bungalow. Between us we furnished it, and there they lived until
half a year later we took Sandy down to Calcutta to meet his far-
out relations, when Margaret was on the first stage of her journey
home.

I had been in touch with a Church of Scotland orphanage for
children of mixed blood, and had asked what they would do about
the boy's future, and had been more than a little disappointed, and
even affronted, at their response. I don't know why I always seem
to be falling out with the powers that be.

But with the war on (Japan wasn't in it yet or things might have
been different), and with the family at home, and news coming of
the blitz and the Battle of Britain, I decided I would be more use
elsewhere. The war wasn't touching us, though we had stepped
up parades of the SVLH just in case.

I wrote to my employers asking again if I could be released for
military service of some sort or another, or if I could be released
from my contract altogether so that I could go home. This was in
mid-1940. They told me it was all right since they weren't going
to renew my contract anyway.

Suburbia and the villages of Jane Austen's day were models of
Christian charity compared with British India – or at least when
compared with a few of the Britons who were in it. Stories spread
and as they spread they grow. The couple who had reported my
communion service were still at large. We had been very friendly
in the beginning and then we had found them out. The rest of the
valley had been wondering how long it would take. They were the
mischief makers, though there was not a great deal to make mischief
about.

I had glowing references from the colonel of the regiment and
from the regular adjutant and others, which should have got me
a commission without any bother. The planters were considering

putting me forward as their representative on the government in Shillong. I should have told them of the ITA's letter and I know they would have taken up the cudgels on my behalf in no uncertain manner. But I'm afraid I'm a person who is easily hurt. I decided to go. Unfortunately I omitted to tell the Bengal Presbytery that I was going.

Maybe this was understandable since I had not been inducted by the Presbytery. There was nothing to be inducted to. So further trouble ensued as the sparks fly upwards.

Two of the senior bachelor planters, with whom I had spent a good deal of time after Margaret left, came down to Calcutta with me after I had sold such contents of the bungalow as belonged to me.

Without telling me, they had secured the signatures of all the planters in the Balisera valley, and in Calcutta got these inscribed on a magnificent silver cigarette box. It's so magnificent that I've never been able to fill it. They saw me to the boat. It was a Dutch tramp of the Holland-Africa line, and there was only one other passenger: a Dundee Jute wallah, and a very decent chap, who departed to his bunk in anything but a dead flat calm. We had very few of these in the three months we were at sea.

The officers and I got on very well together, though the captain had a passion for Monopoly, which is a game I loathe. The doctor was a Czech who'd had to get out before he was put in the bag. He had some Jewish blood. He told me in an expansive moment that I was the first intelligent Englishman he had met. I told him that he had been moving in the wrong circles and that there were a few Scotsmen who were as intelligent as I was.

We had a couple of days in Durban and a couple in Cape Town, and landed at Oban in a snowstorm. I didn't have a coat, and it was a Sunday. There was one bus for Glasgow. We caught it and arrived pretty well frozen. Margaret was living in digs in Largs. There was one bus for Largs. I caught it, and reached that Ayrshire holiday resort more or less numb. I knew the address but hadn't the faintest idea where it was. It was still snowing, and it was the black-out. I found a phone box and got in touch with the police. I described the predicament. They gave me directions; first on the right, second on the left, and so on and so forth. At this point

I interrupted the desk sergeant and explained that three months ago I had left India's sunny clime, and was now shivering on Greenland's icy mountains. I had two suitcases bulging with the exotic splendours of the Far East, but I hadn't an overcoat. Could he send a police car or get me a taxi, or a hearse or something. He sent a police car and landed me at the garden gate about midnight.

There was no glimmer of light on earth or sky. Just the snow, which was falling, it appeared, eternally. I rang the doorbell. After some minutes I rang it again.

A tremulous voice sounded from within inquiring who was without. I asked if this was where Mrs Dow resided, and was informed that this was indeed so. I asked the voice to inform Margaret that her long-lost husband had arrived. I was admitted among scenes which baffle description. They were half expecting me, wife, daughter and wife's older sister. But not at midnight on a Sunday. In preparation for my impending arrival they were all wearing curlers. When the door was opened by the trembling landlady they were all trying unsuccessfully to get rid of the curlers. The landlady was also wearing curlers, but she let them be since she was not expecting a husband home from India. Or from anywhere else for that matter.

Mother at that time was living in Largs too, as was Margaret's younger sister Helen, whose husband was in the Army. Next day the reunions took place. Later the in-laws had to be visited in Paisley and the presents distributed. When these necessary offices had been performed I went to see the Presbytery clerk of Paisley whom I knew of old. He asked for my certificates, and I asked him what certificates. It was as bad as the couple who had turned up to get married on that Friday night in Glasgow.

The certificates had to be got from Calcutta, so to Calcutta I wrote, and that takes some time. In the meantime I would have another bash at the Army. I procured one of the eyesight-testing cards and memorized it. I put in my application and was bidden to appear at the recruiting station in Paisley.

Everything went fine till I went into the room for the eye test. A chap wearing a white coat was sitting at a desk, and I thought I could bluff him. He looked up. It was our family doctor who had brought me into the world some thirty-three years previously. He asked me what I was doing where I was. I told him. I wanted to join the Army.

I had been naked when he had first seen me, and still was. He said 'Not with your eyesight, Jimmy,' and then inquired how Mother and the rest of the family were getting on. And they lament the passing of the family doctor!

He suggested that I might try the Intelligence Corps, where, it seemed, intelligence was valued above mere eyesight. I applied, mentioning some knowledge of Hindustani (I did not mention Latin, Greek or Hebrew) as a possibility. They sent me to a chap who must have spent a lifetime in India as a missionary, and he proceeded to ask me questions in a language which he assured me was Hindustani, but which bore as little resemblance to the Hindi I spoke as Oxbridge English bears to the variety spoken in the Gallowgate. I hadn't the faintest idea what he was talking about, and I think this was mutual. I returned to Largs and joined Dad's Army.

26. And so to Greenock

In the meantime came word from Calcutta that the Presbytery were holding back a certificate just to be a lesson to me. The Paisley Presbytery clerk said that this was all wrong and that he would deal with it. I told him not to bother. It was only for another year, and I had other thoughts anyway. I was more than beginning to wonder if the ministry was the job for me. What about journalism?

I went to the Labour Exchange in Largs, but they were not looking for journalists. And I wasn't a member of the union anyway. The only work they could offer which was connected even remotely with the war effort was house-painting. The name of Dow plainly did not mean anything at all. And no wonder. It's different today, in Scotland anyway. I can't go anywhere without hearing somebody whisper to somebody else, with a significant glance in my direction: 'There's Dow that you see on the telly.'

I was in the gents' room of a restaurant one day, and the attendant approached me with the words: 'Speak, and I will tell you who you are.' I assured him that I knew who I was even without speaking.

Going through Central Station one day I was stopped by an elderly chap who held out his hand. He asked if he might shake hands with me. I said that I would be delighted and honoured. We chatted for a little while, and then I pointed out that I was going for my train.

He told me that he and his wife never missed me on radio or television. I was easily their favourite broadcaster. He couldn't get home quick enough to tell his wife that he had shaken hands (and he looked at his right hand as if he had made up his mind that he would never wash it again) with the Reverend James Currie, who is a very good friend of mine.

But it was all so different in 1941. Then I was an unknown, and was beginning to feel that an unknown I would remain for the rest of my days on earth.

F*

I got in touch with the clerk of Pulpit Supply who told me he could keep me employed every Sunday. The holding back of the certificate made no difference to that. Then a chap came along (he was a Roman Catholic, who had evacuated his family to West Kilbride, and didn't want to send them to the local school). He asked me if I would give them lessons every morning. I said I would. Another chap came along who worked with the Ministry of Information, and asked if I would lecture for them. I said I would. The war effort, I'm afraid, was mainly Dad's Army.

It may be a bit of a joke, Dad's Army, but those who, like me, served in it know that we would have given a pretty good account of ourselves, and I believe I could have taken as many along with me as I had shells in the magazine of the excellent Ross rifle supplied by Canada.

I've always had an old Scots philosophy which can't quite be translated into the English, that 'what's for ye will nae gae by ye'. I hold that philosophy more strongly now than I did then, though I can't say that at that time I felt very confident or very happy about the future.

The clerk of Pulpit Supply sent me down to Trinity Church in the Ayrshire town of Irvine. It was a fine church, with fine people in it. I took to them and they took to me. Their minister was an army chaplain.

After the first service I conducted (I don't know if it was the trial of St Paul or the mountains of the Bible, but I'll lay a bet it was one or the other) the officebearers gathered round and asked me if it was possible for me to come every Sunday, and if I could possibly come down on the Friday afternoon and visit the sick and the old folk. They made a reasonable offer for the service, and I asked them if they were deducting this from their minister's stipend. They assured me that they were not, and I agreed to come. I enjoyed every minute of it, and got on with the Irvine folk famously.

Irvine, Paisley, and Greenock all claim to have the oldest Burns Club in the world. I am bard of the Greenock club, and an honorary member of Irvine. I don't know what Paisley is thinking about.

A good many troops, especially commandos, were stationed in and around Irvine, and the YMCA ran a canteen for them. I got involved in this, and in some way became their unofficial chaplain.

One Sunday a man appeared in the vestry and introduced himself to me. He was an officebearer in Cartsburn Augustine Church in Greenock, which was vacant. They had heard of me. I asked him if they had heard everything about me. He said he didn't know, so I explained about the certificate and told him it might arrive any minute. I asked him if the Greenock church had a manse. He said it had not. And this was what Margaret and I had been looking for.

This was not the first congregation that had come to hear me, but I had to express uninterest. We had no furniture and, apart from the fact that you couldn't get furniture, we weren't going into the HP market again. I told him that if they would arrange a date for me to preach I would preach, and they could take it from there. Which they did, and so my real ministry began, and continued in Greenock for the next twenty-three years.

There's a wee story connected with this. It is a regulation of the Church of Scotland that when a minister is called to a charge all minutes and transactions of the vacancy committee must be destroyed.

The clerk to this vacancy committee was a most efficient lassie who was secretary to a local industrialist, and her minutes were an absolute model of what minutes should be. The committee must have thought it would be almost blasphemous to consign such perfection to the boiler fire. I found the document at the bottom of a drawer, and without any pang of conscience read it.

There had been applications (not many, for Cartsburn Augustine was no great catch). There had been hearings, there had been disappointments. There had been confustion of counsel.

Then there followed the report by Peter Macduff (whose wife was daughter of my predecessor in that church) of his visit to Irvine and of his impression of myself. The matter of the missing certificate had been discussed at some length. Inquiries had been made at Barony North, my first charge. The inquirers had been told that I was a fine chap, excellent with young people, a first-class preacher, but an unenthusiastic visitor except to the housebound.

On the occasion when the kirk session thought I should visit all the members for the second time (I have referred to this earlier), I was able to tell them that before they called me to Greenock they had received a testimonial that I was not an enthusiastic visitor, and that it was their own fault. This was received in the spirit in which it was offered: with considerable hilarity.

On Saturday before I preached as sole nominee I was staying with the interim moderator, John Graham of Crawfurdsburn, which was to the east of Cartsburn. After lunch I could see that he was restless. When the sound of many voices was heard in the neighbourhood about three o'clock, he appeared more restless.

Being rather quick at these things I asked him if he was yearning to go to Cappielow, the ground of the Greenock Morton football club. He said that he was. I said that so was I. We got ready, and went.

When we arrived, about half an hour after the kick-off, Morton were beating Clyde two nothing. Maybe it was our arrival that did it, maybe not. But at full time Clyde had won three two. For the next twenty years I was a season-ticket holder.

In the absence of the manse which we wanted, the next thing to do was to find a furnished house, and that was no easy task in wartime Greenock. In the meantime we continued to live in Largs, and now that the future seemed rather more settled than it had been, a second baby was on the way, and due at the end of May.

Eventually we found a splendid top flat of a substantial villa in the west end of the town. And the west end of Greenock is a splendid place to live in. It belonged to an elderly lady who was going to live with her daughter, and I think she must have taken a notion to us. The seven-roomed house, with three attics, was ours for three pounds a week.

My stipend was £450 a year; so after paying the rent we had six pounds a week to live on, which wasn't all that much. There was no allowance for the telephone, travelling expenses, postage, or anything else. But Cartsburn was beginning to prosper.

I was lucky to follow James Francis, who had been there for twenty-five years and who was a real character. During the depression Greenockians from the east end used to camp out down the coast, and he was their chaplain, known as the Bishop of Lunderston Bay. But the blitz had wrought havoc with the east end. The congregation was scattered, and congregations always fall away during a vacancy. But they were coming back. A great deal of Sunday work was being done in the yards, and most of my men were in the yards and engine shops. I started a service at eight o'clock on Sunday nights to accommodate them, and I will say that the men responded. There's a verse which goes:

> The Church of Scotland is a place
> Fairly full of life.
> Where you'll find the Scottish working man
> Represented by his wife.

It isn't very good poetry but it's very true. I tried to mend this, for I had a theory, and indeed still have it, though it's a conviction now; if you want to get a family interested in the church, you've got to get Father interested. There's no use Mother flyting at the family on a Sunday morning to get out to church if the old man's lying in his bed reading the *News of the World*.

The Women's Guild was doing fine under Margaret's ministrations, and there was a very active afternoon meeting for women. There was nothing for men. And in the pre-television era and during the War people were looking for somewhere to go, and for something to do o' nights. I wrote to every man on the roll. I had already written to all those who were on active service. I invited them to a meeting in the church hall.

There were two halls, but the larger one had been taken over as a gas cleansing station and was unusable. The response was very good indeed. Nearly all the fellows knew one another, but in case any didn't I invited each to stand up, identify himself, and tell us what he did for a living. We discussed the possibility of starting a Men's Guild, and they seemed enthusiastic. A minister (or anybody else, for that matter) is wasting his time and energy if he tries to start anything for which there is no demand.

We appointed officebearers, we discussed various activities. I suggested a St Andrew's supper. Like most Scots who have not been abroad they didn't know when St Andrew's Day was. I would prepare the meal. They looked doubtful, not then knowing Dow's culinary prowess. I don't think their imagination rose above pies. But they decided we should have a St Andrew's Day supper.

One of the female members of the church was in charge of Scott's, the shipbuilders, canteen. I asked her if she would seek official permission to lend me crockery, cutlery, and pots. She did so, and permission was readily granted.

Another member was a fishmonger and I approached him in the matter of salt herring. The butcher said he could provide haggis without ration cards. Vegetables and potatoes were not difficult, and bones for the soup were available. I also managed to get the ingredients for a clootie dumpling. Which, to the uninitiated, is a Christmas pudding in a cloth. The menu was:

Scotch broth (that the spoon could stand up in)

Salt herring

Haggis, mashed potato and turnip

Dumpling with custard

Tea, oatcakes and cheese

The supper was a resounding success. In fact, with some of them it was still resounding three days later. There was only one slight snag, and I learned this later from the canteen manageress: next day she had complaints that the mince tasted of herring.

But this, and other ideas, got the men well and truly within the fold. Sunday attendances got better and better, and the offerings improved. At a board meeting I asked if they would reduce my pay and in turn pay for the house. They asked me to leave the meeting and then informed me that they would pay for the house without reducing the stipend. Some years later the old lady who owned the house died, and her daughter offered the house to the church at a very reasonable figure. We floated a loan and bought it. Margaret and I bought the furniture.

When I went to Cartsburn there were only about eight elders, all middle-aged. The majority of the enthusiastic men were on the congregational board, which is the finance court of the church. I wanted them as elders and I told the kirk session so. They smiled cynically and told me they had been trying for years without success. I didn't lay any bets but I told them I would get fifteen new elders. This time they laughed scornfully.

We published a monthly magazine, which I wrote, and which was a fairly light-hearted affair, though often I had to record events which were very far from being light-hearted. But I'm afraid I'm like the man who said that he wanted to be a philosopher, but humour was always breaking through.

In this magazine I announced the intention to increase the kirk session by fifteen, and said that very soon voting papers would be distributed, containing the name and address of every man on the roll, each with a wee square for his vote – if any.

I then made a list of the twelve reasons for not accepting the eldership, which I expected to get when I came round after the voting. These ranged from 'I'm not good enough' to 'I haven't got a frock-coat'. Each of the reasons I demolished in print.

There was a heavy poll, and I set off to see the men who had been voted in, though I made it clear that nobody but myself would know who the first fifteen were. I didn't want any man to feel that he was playing as substitute. I had practically no bother. Some of them merely confessed that they couldn't think up any reason for refusing that I hadn't already disposed of. All they could do was surrender.

27. New Doors Open

This started a very happy relationship which lasted for more than twenty years. The former session clerk – the chap I had to shake hands with – had left, and we decided to learn a lesson and to appoint an official for a limited number of years: five. And he was not what they call in Scotland 'illegible' for re-election.

By this method, of course, you lose a good man after five years, but this is more than compensated for by the fact that you don't have to put up with a bad one for any longer.

Soon I found myself becoming involved in activities outside the church, and for this my predecessor was largely responsible, for Jimmy Francis had been very much involved and I was supposed to follow in his footsteps. Among his offices was the chaplaincy of the Orange Lodge, but this I gracefully declined not being Irish.

There are, of course, a multitude of organizations engaged in good works, and good luck to them. I have never been a member of any of them because I have always felt that I am a member of the greatest of them all: the Christian Church. The members of these organizations will tell you that there could be no finer way of life than that laid down by their constitution if only their members would live up to it. There is always this 'if only' and that goes for membership of the church just as assuredly.

James Francis had also been a Burns enthusiast, as a very large number of Greenockians are. Before very long I was invited to propose the Immortal Memory at the St John's Club.

Maybe I would have been wiser to refuse the invitation from the St John's Club, for it started something that has gone on ever since and which has taken me all over Scotland from Peterhead to Dumfries, and all over England from Kent to Leeds, and even over to Belfast. They even ask me back. I tell them that I have only one Immortal Memory and have no intention ever to write another one. When you have produced the best that you believe yourself capable of, anything else is only second best.

However, I acquired a reputation, and found myself being invited further and further afield. On one occasion when I was to perform before the London Caledonian Society, Frazer McLusky, minister of Pont Street, asked me to preach there, since I would be staying over the weekend anyway. Please do not think that I was neglecting my duties by doing this. A minister is entitled to four Sundays off in the year at the congregation's expense and I took only two weeks off, which I spent cooking for the Boys' Brigade camp.

Before going to London I'd been at half a dozen local Burns suppers, toasting the lasses, reciting *Tam o' Shanter* and addressing the haggis, of whose sonsy face I had seen just about enough.

In St Columba's, Pont Street, they have a lunch after service for those who have come a distance. It's a big church, and they drape a microphone round your neck which you plug in when it's your turn to make your contribution to the service. While you're waiting for your moment you sit on the side-lines.

And there I was sitting when there came, wafted through the ventilating system, the aroma of haggis and turnip, which was being prepared in the kitchen down below. It gave me an introduction to my remarks, which appeared to be appreciated even by the respectable and successful Scots who constitute that splendid congregation. This was more than I could say for the lunch. But this was years and years ahead.

I was to become a great deal more involved with the community, however, before very long.

As I may have said in an earlier chapter, in Greenock there was a dividing line between the east end and the west end. My real introduction to the west end, apart from the fact that we lived there and knew the neighbours, was when I was invited to address the '43 Club.

This consisted originally of corporation officials who had been brought together in the organization of civil defence, but its membership had expanded quite a bit. They met once a fortnight in Mackay's

tea rooms at teatime, and heard a paper on some subject or another –
usually highly controversial. They then proceeded to tear the speaker
apart. No holds were barred, and it was always very good-humoured.

The club was really a cross section of the managerial and professional side of the community. This was before Rotary had come
on the scene in the town.

I was invited to speak and took the Gollancz theme: 'Our
threatened values'. I never miss a chance to preach a sermon. I
managed to hold my own in the wordy exchanges which followed,
and in the club I made acquaintanceships which soon ripened into
friendships. These connections were very useful, though by no means
profitable in any physical way. Talking to my own churchmen I
got the worker's point of view and the foreman's point of view. In
the '43 Club I got another point of view, and I'm a good listener.
I will sit at the feet of any man who knows more than I do about
any matter.

After the listening there comes the analysis, and that means
putting the two points of view together. Or rather the three points
of view, for foremen have their own. They've a hard, hard row to
hoe. I very soon came to the conclusion that the main trouble with
local industry (and if this applied to Greenock and Port Glasgow
it surely applied anywhere and everywhere) was that men were
inhibited with 'the two sides of industry', when the fact is that there
is only one.

Mentally they may have agreed with Kipling that 'East is East
and West is West and never the twain shall meet'; but there's another
line: 'Till two strong men stand face to face, before the judgement
seat.'

Of course in some ways it was understandable enough, especially
in the east end. Memories of the Depression were still vivid, and
especially of the vicious means test. And I had a strong suspicion
during those War years that many of the bosses were sighing nostalgically for the good old days when there were two men looking
for every one job. Not that they ever admitted it, of course. But the
more I talked with 'one side' and then with the 'other side' I was
convinced that unless the chance given by the War was grabbed
with both hands, the twenty years after it would be no better, and
could even be worse, than the twenty years before it.

The same was true of the corporation, which Labour had recently taken control of for the first time. The opposition consisted of Moderates, Independents, and Progressives. But they had brought this on themselves, since, being among the higher ratepayers, it was obviously to their advantage to keep local rates as low as possible.

The working men, of course, had wrong ideas too. Many of them had discovered that there is such a thing as income tax, and this came as a surprise bordering on a shock. They still thought the fair and proper way to run a country was to soak the rich for the sake of the poor. Make the capitalist pay. They conveniently forget that every time they fill up a football coupon they are dreaming of being capitalists.

The working man is seldom a good payer-out; something which probably stems from the time when he didn't have very much to pay out. Our offerings in Cartsburn, Sunday by Sunday, and with good attendances, were nothing like what they should have been. With a few honourable exceptions the majority were giving about half of what they could have given.

One day there arrived in Greenock a new assistant to a Church Extension charge: George Wilkie, who is now head of the Department on Industrial Chaplaincies. He had his ideas about how the church could bring together 'the two sides of industry'. We called a meeting, but it was more a confrontation. Nobody would commit himself. They had come with their built-in prejudices. They were all on the defensive.

I had spoken both publicly and privately to my men, urging them to play a full and active part in the unions. I asked them why they didn't offer themselves for election as shop stewards. Most of them never even attended a branch meeting. They paid their dues and that was all. But they soon made their reasons clear.

The union delegate and the shop steward who was doing his job were marked men. They knew more about this than I did. They knew that when they went upstairs to see the manager or director they would not be received as fellow members of the church; they would not be received as fellow elders. The only communication was an industrial communication, for this was the only level they met on. And most of them on both sides were decent chaps all, who met and were very friendly when one bowling club played another.

So the Christian Industrial Fellowship was started, and it was a complete flop. When I say the managements were mainly responsible for this I'm not excusing the men, for they were anything but enthusiastic. The truth of it is that people do not want to meet as Christians; it demands too much, and they don't want to be embarrassed.

It's the same with people who say: 'I don't go to church because the church has nothing to say.' Who do they think they're kidding? The church has too much to say, and they know that what the church has to say is the truth. And they can't take it. They would have to commit themselves, and that's the last thing to do. It's demanding, it's disturbing, and the annoying thing is that it's right – and they know it.

Jesus was crucified, not because they thought he was wrong but because they knew he was right, and didn't dare admit it because of the consequences to their cherished way of life. When the truth confronts you and you can't take it, the best thing to do is to get rid of it. And that is why there is so little peace in industry: because there is so little truth.

Anyway, in Greenock new doors were opening for me. Maybe the reason why they had never opened before was that I had never knocked on them before. I found a door and I knocked, and it opened and has stayed open these thirty years.

Greenock has rather an unusual newspaper: the *Greenock Telegraph*.

I wrote to the owner and managing editor, R. J. Erskine Orr, and offered a short weekly article, which I titled 'Design for Living'. It was a kind of topical sermon, or a combination of sermon and children's address. He asked me to come and see him, which I did. He liked the content and the style.

Because of the demands of war the paper was very short-staffed both on the reporting and the editorial side. Erskine Orr wrote the leading articles, but he was away a bit, and busy with other things. The leader devolved on the chief reporter who had plenty on his plate already.

He asked Mr Orr if occasionally when he was pushed he could ask me to write the leader. This was agreed. One day he phoned and asked if I would come to the office in the morning and write. I arrived about half past nine and learned that the leader had to be ready for the compositor at eleven. I asked what I was supposed to write about, and was told 'about eight hundred words'.

I made the deadline with many alterations, erasures and corrections. As time went on these became fewer, and the writing quicker. Of course, when an article which is the last to be locked up in the forme is written it is written. You can change literals in proof, but nothing else. You get it right first time or it stays wrong. And this is a very valuable discipline. And the leading article can't be written the day before and then polished up, unless it is on an item of news which came in after the paper had gone to bed.

I invited Mr Orr out to our Men's Guild and he was greatly impressed, not only with the quality of the men but with the grasp that I seemed to have of their problems. The result was that he asked me to take on the total job of leader writer, which meant six a week; the Saturday one being, allegedly, humorous. So it was down to the office every morning at the back of nine, and there in the office, between writing the leader and correcting the proof, I wrote my letters and sermons and anything else I had to write.

Greenock in those days was a splendid Presbytery, and could have claimed to be the best in Scotland. We thought so, but we never said so in public. One year the Presbytery appointed a committee to work with representatives of other churches, including the Roman Catholic, and some members of the corporation, to draw up the first Code for Citizens ever to be published in Britain. It was a short, thoughtful and stimulating document, but, alas, I fear it has made little difference to the community's way of life. There are those in every town who do not need any such document to tell them their civic and public responsibilities. And there are those who do need it but never read it.

28. A Touch of Drama

Whatever relations between Protestant and Roman Catholic clergy may be, or may have been in other towns, in Greenock they were very cordial.

John Daniel was priest of St Laurence's, about a couple of hundred yards up the hill from Cartsburn, and he and I got on very well together.

The old St Laurence's had been blitzed, and when the new one had been built and opened he invited me up to see it. He showed me round, but I can't say I was greatly impressed. I was wondering all the time what this edifice had cost. We examined the rooms of the junior priests, then went up to John's quarters, which can be described only as palatial. He opened the cocktail cabinet and asked what I would like, and I said that seeing where I was, a drop of the Auld Kirk would be seemly. He had a gin and tonic, and we sat down before a splendid log fire. Outside a sleety rain was falling, and stealing up the stairs there was the aroma of a roast of beef.

'Aye, aye, James,' he said at last, lying back and stretching out his feet. 'You married men have a lot to be thankful for too.'

I nodded agreement, trying to remember if it was mince or sliced sausage we were having for lunch.

We talked about many things, and the conversation turned to the Presbytery. We were having trouble trying to negotiate a union between two vacant congregations, which is always a most difficult job. John Daniel said: 'The Presbytery must stick to its guns. Of course,' he went on, 'we're in a better position than you are. We can always appeal in the end of the day to the Pope. You have only God, and a lot of your people don't accept His authority.'

I became friendly too with a number of the junior priests, for we were working in the same parish after all, especially with John Boyle. I suggested a football match. He thought it might be rather dangerous in Greenock, a Rangers-Celtic encounter. But I assured him that my intention was exactly the opposite. This team would be ecumenical: a combined team of ministers and priests against the press. How many could he raise? He guaranteed five, I was to supply the other six.

We arranged to have the use of Cappielow, and on the night of the game the place was packed. Four of the priests were in the forward line and one in goal; the defence was Presbyterian. We beat the press six nothing. When Roman Catholics pointed out in the yards that all the goals had been scored by the priests, the Protestants pointed out that the defence had been the ministers. The Catholics then reminded them that the goalkeeper was a priest whereupon they were reminded that he didn't have to save a shot all night.

Sam Leitch, now of the BBC Sports Department, was a reporter with the *Greenock Telegraph* at that time. He played centre for the press and I played centre half. Which speaks for itself.

Later on, the *Telegraph* staff who'd been in the forces began to come back, and it became a question of what was to happen to Dow? They didn't want to get rid of me, but the regular leader writer was one of the returned soldiers. Mr Orr suggested that I should do a weekly article under the name of Our Industrial Correspondent.

The idea was that when any industrial disputation arose (and there was no shortage of these after the War) I would investigate, interview, and report. It was all very interesting and very revealing. Nobody would talk.

It struck me then that the reason why they said nothing was that they had practically nothing to say. The case was so weak when it was closely scrutinized. They were scared to have it written up by one who was unbiased and who was known to have a sense of humour. I could get nothing out of managements and even less out of trade union officials. Sometimes, though, I felt I was getting somewhere.

The railwaymen in one dispute were working to rule, so off I went to discover what working to rule really meant. About the only thing out of the past that wasn't mentioned was the need to have a man with a red flag walking in front of the engine. I suggested that the rules might be altered, but learned that compared with the railway regulations, the laws of the Medes and the Persians were mere tentative suggestions.

A nightwatchman approached me about the wages and conditions they worked under. I wrote the thing up and an improvement was effected. A boilermaker whom I knew spoke to me about the way riveters were paid, which was a relic of the days when the ganger contracted for the job and then paid the money out to the gang in a public house. After my article on the subject the method of payment was changed and I got a letter of thanks from the society.

But it was hard going, and then I discovered that some of my church lads, especially foremen and under-foremen, were not at all popular with their managements, who knew who the Industrial Correspondent was and who wanted to know where he was getting his information. Anybody who went around with his eyes and ears open could get the same information.

The secretary of one firm told me he had stopped speaking to me. I told him he was breaking my heart, and that anything he had ever said when he was speaking to me wasn't worth listening to. But I couldn't see my men getting into trouble.

On one occasion after the launch of a ship from a yard now defunct, there was the usual lunch and the *Telegraph* reported the usual managerial speech which in those days was all 'Woe, woe, what are we going to do now?' The fact of the matter was that the contract for the next job was usually already signed. It just wasn't the opportune time to announce it to their workers, who had to be first persuaded that the yard was on the brink of bankruptcy. I wrote that this yard really ought to have a built-in wailing wall to be used on launching days. They took the matter up with Mr Orr who called me to his room and told me that perhaps I had gone a little too far. Next day he called me again to his room and showed me a letter from the chairman of the federation which said that it was high time somebody said something of the kind. So all was well.

But shortly afterwards the industrial column ceased upon the midnight with no pain. It wasn't that we were scared of it: just that I couldn't get the material. And Albert Harbour was born.

The title came from the name of one of Greenock's harbours,

and there was another called the Victoria Harbour which allowed Albert to have a wife.

When some time later it was impossible to hide behind the name and Greenockians had learned who I was, my wife was frequently addressed as Victoria. The off-beat adventures of Albert and Victoria became very popular and went on for years till we moved to Arran. You can't write Greenock humour at that distance. In case any of the *Telegraph* directors buy this book, or borrow it from somebody, I make the suggestion that it's time they published *The Best of Albert Harbour,* before the column is forgotten altogether.

But there came a day when the assistant editor left for another job. He had been writing the leaders, and I was appointed to fill the vacancy, but still with Albert Harbour on my lap. There were still two more doors to open for me in Greenock – drama and broadcasting. I must have been a late developer.

With the War over, the church hall had been restored to its proper uses. We got the Boys' Brigade going again, and a Youth Club. The Life Boys and Guides and Brownies had managed to keep going in the small hall. We started a drama club.

Greenock, even then, was a namely place for drama, though the clubs had not quite risen to the heights they have since attained. But the drama was booming. People were looking for somewhere to go and for something to do. There was, of course, no television. We got a fairly competent group together, and there was plenty of back-stage help.

The first show was the old Scots classic *Bunty Pulls the Strings,* and we followed this with some of Tim Watson's kitchen comedies (and what's wrong with kitchen comedies?), including *Beneath the Wee Red Lums* and *Bachelors Are Bold.* This was the kind of stuff that people wanted to be entertained with, and the main purpose of drama is entertainment. Tragedy can be entertainment too. The Elizabethans went to see *King Lear* because they wanted to be entertained, not because they wanted to be educated.

Drama clubs can put on what they think the public *ought* to want to see, and then complain because the public don't want to see it. But if you charge admission at the box office you've got to put on what the public want to see, and you've got to do it very well. When you don't, you get an empty house.

I had already written a number of sketches and things for the Women's Guild and the Men's Guild, but I got the notion of trying my hand at a full-length play. This would not have to be submitted to another club or a publisher. What's the use of having a club of your own unless you can get your own work played?

The Greenock Arts Guild (and I must say something about this rare organization later) organized a competition for churches' and works' drama clubs in full-length plays. We reached the final and would have won that if we had played as well as we had in the previous round. It bears out the old adage that if you make a thing better you spoil it, when it was good enough the way it was.

One of the adjudicators was Ray Linn Craig, one of the best, if not the best, amateur producers in Scotland. She must have detected some latent talent in me, for she invited me to join her club – the Greenock Players, and there I learned a great deal about acting, production and the construction of plays. But my first loyalty was always to the church club.

I wrote a full-length comedy for them, *Loot Goes North*, which was later played by the Greenock Players as *Highland Gathering*, and a number of one-act plays as well.

Good religious plays are in short supply, and in most of them the players dress themselves up in bedsheets and speak Authorized Version English. I wrote a couple.

One was called *Kingston Hotel*. It struck me when I was thinking about a nativity play that if Joseph and Mary couldn't get into the inn because it was full, then it was full of their own relatives, however far out. For they had all come to Bethlehem because they 'were of the tribe and lineage of David'. We played it in modern dress with the Russians taking the place of the Romans. Another was *Occupied Territory*, which was the Upper Room played in a modern setting. In it appeared as a small boy, playing the part of John Mark, one Bill Bryden who is fast making a name for himself as producer and writer for stage and television. When his first play, *Willie Rough,* was done at the Edinburgh Lyceum, Bill graciously acknowledged in an interview the small part I had played in his career.

Then my organist Robert Goodwin, a brilliant organist and pianist, decided to start a junior choir and put on shows. But the kind of score and libretto for this kind of thing is very limited, so we saw that if we wanted anything better we would have to do it ourselves. I wrote the words, Robert wrote the music. It was quite a Gilbert and Sullivan act.

Our first was *Aladdin*, and I was told by one critic it was the first time he had seen *Aladdin* without Widow Twankey. The second was more ambitious. It was called *The Tale of the Bank*. It started in the stone age and went on scene by scene till we were going into space. The illusion was to be created by fixing rockets to a bicycle wheel nailed on to a board in the wings. Unfortunately the rockets were not tied tightly enough, and there was quite an unrehearsed scene, without, I am happy to say, any harm being done.

Greenock Arts Guild was another 'first' in Scotland. Greenock has a remarkably large number of firsts. In the west end were the disused west end baths (a natural place for them to be). A small band of enthusiasts bought the building and with help from various sources including the Arts Council and Greenock Corporation converted it, first into a small theatre upstairs, holding about a hundred and twenty, and then, when they saw that success was assured, the former pond was made into a splendid theatre holding about four hundred. Which is just about the ideal for a town theatre.

The first show was a rather depressing Norwegian play; the second was my *Tale of the Bank*, which went like a bomb, with all the talent of Greenock taking part in it. And Greenock has some of the best dramatic talent and some of the best choirs in Scotland. After this I found myself becoming even more drawn into things, and especially into the Greenock Players, which was very enjoyable but rather time-consuming. Extra rehearsals had to be held late so that I could be there, for the Players were heading for the big time.

In Colin Maclean's *The Reeve's Tale* (Chaucer in Scots verse) we won our district, then division, then the Scottish final, which meant a trip to London to represent our native land. We won. Greenock Players reached the national final again a few years later but this time were not placed first. I was not in that one, but there is no connection between the two facts.

Then Ray Linn Craig, the producer, asked me if I would write another Chaucer-based one-act play as *The Reeve's Tale* had done so well. I wrote *The Miller's Tale* which I called *Tail-piece* for obvious reasons. There was a red-hot ploughshare involved in the original. We made do with a red-hot poker. It was a big cast, consisting of almost all the guests in the Tabard Inn, which was the scene of the play.

Ray will not mind, I know, if I pass on a hint to young producers. We played on a stage constructed on the stage. This meant that wherever we were, and whatever size the stage was, we played on the same size of stage as we had done last time.

Before the curtain went up, all the Canterbury Pilgrims were in position in the Tabard Inn. But the stage was dark, I was in the wings in a little box with a light above me. I was a schoolmaster, correcting essays on Chaucer, and I spoke a prologue. I can't remember all the lines, and I haven't a copy of it to remind me.

One couplet was:

> They don't read Chaucer for the language's glories;
> They only read Chaucer for the dirtier stories.

It was obvious before the prologue was ended that we had the audience in our hands if we could deal with them. We won the Scottish and headed for Wales for the British final, which was, of course, against the winners of the English, Welsh and Irish festivals. They were all serious plays, and it was plain that the audience was becoming bored.

They hadn't had a laugh all night, and during the prologue I got laughs in the most unexpected places. That was the mood they were in. When my light went out and the lights slowly came on on the stage, the audience burst out clapping, for it was quite a picture. Then off it went at the speed comedy should be played. We had the lot, with the old chap being pulled up in the tub in case there was a flood, and it ended with the red-hot poker.

According to the audience there was no doubt who was the winner, and the adjudicator agreed. His adjudication of one of the clubs (I won't say which, though the scars must have healed by this time) was that he had seen that play at least twenty times and this was the worst performance he'd had to sit through.

I was at camp with my Boys' Brigade at Glenluce at the time, and joined the club bus at Gretna. I brought one of my pipers to Wales.

The moment the verdict was announced Hugh broke into 'Scotland the Brave' and continued to the delight of everybody who wasn't trying to make a speech.

To win the British final twice was a record, since equalled by the Players' rival club in Greenock, the George Square Players; indeed, almost surpassed in 1973 when, as finalists, they were placed second, having already won twice.

This drama business didn't all happen at once, of course, but was spread over twenty years. I've just tried to exhaust the subject all at once, at the risk of exhausting the reader.

There was still something to come, however. I wrote *Graham Came by Cleish* (now published by Jarrolds of London as a novel) and entered it for the SCDA full-length play competition, which it won. The Greenock Players gave it its première in the Arts Guild Theatre, with myself playing John Pitcairn. As I said in another place, that is why John Pitcairn has all the best lines.

It lost by a short neck in the national competition for full-length plays. I told them it must have been in the playing, for it couldn't possibly have been in the writing. It was played later on the Edinburgh Festival fringe, but I think we did it better. Adjudicators can be very funny. They can be very unfunny too, but they can be very funny.

Howard M. Lockhart of the BBC was adjudicating *Graham Came by Cleish,* and he's an old acquaintance of mine. He knew that I did not have a limp. I limped all through the play, and in his public adjudication Howard pointed out to young players how well this had been done. Many actors, he said, adopted some kind of gimmick and then forgot. But Dow, he said, had not forgotten. He had started with a limp and he had ended with a limp.

What Howard didn't know, till I told him afterwards, was that a fortnight before I had burst my Achilles tendon and was just waiting to go into hospital to have it sewn together. It's a wonder I didn't finish the play on the flat of my back. It was sheer agony. But the play must go on.

Later the BBC in Scotland promoted a television play competition, and I was in the first three. The only thing they didn't like was the ending, which I liked very much. But the man who pays the piper calls the tune. I changed it. The play was produced and went down rather well. But I still think the original ending was better.

My last appearance on the stage in Greenock was in a combined clubs show where I played Falstaff in *The Merrie Wives of Windsor*. The *Daily Mail* drama critic wrote that it was the first time he had heard Falstaff played with a Scots accent.

29. On the Air

Life can't be divided into compartments. Everything in life is related. Interest in drama and in writing plays made it clear to me that though I wasn't all that hot at working out plots, I could write dialogue, and make people speak the way people speak.

My knowledge of the Gospels and my feeling for them had made it possible for me to make some parts of them come alive on the stage, and the Bible is full of plots. All it needs is the dialogue. There are plenty of characters, good and bad, and I found that the best way to make them real was to have a meeting with them, and to talk about their lives and thoughts and dreams.

Dr Macgregor would have approved, I think, for he was an old Free Kirk man, and Thomas Chalmers had used this method in his preaching on occasion. People liked it, and I've used it quite a bit in broadcasting. Of course broadcasting wasn't there in the beginning. It was in the early 1950s that I first sat in front of the microphone. But before I come to that, one other remark about preaching, or public speaking, for preaching is just public speaking with a particular purpose.

In the *Greenock Telegraph* we were not allowed to start any story with the definite or indefinite article. Sometimes you have to stand a sentence on its head to avoid it. But it's a good rule which other larger newspapers might well adopt. Then you wouldn't have a page of articles each starting with 'The'.

Journalism, too, had a great influence on my preaching, and without being immodest I may remark that in the introduction to my book of sermons, called *Late and Early*, Dr William Barclay said that I was one of the great communicators. That's what writing is and that's what speaking is – communication.

But if you're going to communicate you've got to catch your audience with your first sentence. This is especially true in preaching.

Sermon time comes round and the congregation are settling

down, though not necessarily for slumber. Anybody who can sleep
in a Church of Scotland pew deserves it. But just when they are
slipping their Imperial into their mouth (the only sweetmeat un-
officially sanctioned by the kirk) you've got to hit them with something a bit unusual.

Many a man starts with: 'My text this morning is taken from the
such-and-such at such-and-such a verse,' and many get away with
it and do a good job. But if I have a text at all (and texts are very
often just a peg to hang some thoughts on) I introduce it later on.
Another thing that journalism teaches is the need for brevity. A
man can go on as long as he likes so long as he is saying something.
But there is nothing a reader objects to more than padding. It's
easy to pad a sermon.

A sermon, like a feature article, can afford to sag a wee bit in the
middle, but it must start on a high note and end on one. The Amen
at the end of the sermon must come as a surprise to the congregation, so that they say to you afterwards: 'I could have listened for
another half-hour,' which is a black burning lie. Another five
minutes and the impact of the sermon would have gone.

A sermon doesn't conclude. Its implication is: 'There it is, friends,
draw your own conclusion.' This is the way Jesus preached, and I
don't think a preacher should look any further than Him for a
model.

But I had started on about broadcasting.

The *Greenock Telegraph* had a church column which appeared on
Saturdays and which was compiled by John Keane, the reporter
who dated events from the introduction of the fish supper. I don't
suppose John had been inside a church for years, but he did a good
job with very little encouragement. The church complains about
lack of news coverage in the press, but trying to get information
out of ministers is like drawing their back teeth. John did his best.
But with my arrival he gladly surrendered the column to me, be-
lieving (and rightly too) that there was more church news in the
company I kept than there was in the company he kept and in the
places which he frequented.

Unfortunately ninety per cent of what congregations believe
to be news isn't news at all. The press does not exist to oblige
organizations with space on the odd occasion when they want to

advertise something. The press is interested in news, but the news must be reasonably important and must be of some interest to the general reader. I asked Mr Orr if I might have a whole page. All the churches advertised their services in the *Telegraph* on the Saturday. He was a bit doubtful, but agreed.

The church adverts were handed in on Thursday, and on the Friday I went through them all, looking for something interesting. Here would be a congregation having an ordination of elders, and nobody had thought it worthwhile to let the paper know who the men were. We all like to see our name in the paper as long as it isn't in the police column. I would have to telephone the minister to get something which was really news and of interest to all the friends and relations of these men. I had to spend hours on the phone, and at the end of the day write half the page myself. The reader may wonder what this has to do with broadcasting, but that will emerge in due season.

Greenock Presbytery decided to have a teaching mission when for six weeks or so all ministers would preach on the same subject each Sunday: 'Christian honesty' and this kind of thing. Questions would be invited, answers would be provided. A small group was appointed to plan out the course, and I was appointed, naturally enough, publicity officer. I had to winkle out of the members of the group a précis of the Sunday subject and suggestions for Bible reading, so that congregations could be prepared. This I managed by sitting in their studies until they had done their homework.

Greenock, of course, had been the birthplace of J. P. Struthers' magnificent magazine, *The Morning Watch*, which, for religious journalism (directed in part towards children) was far ahead of its time, and which has seldom been equalled and never surpassed. One of the celebrated features of it was 'Reasons for not going to church'. These excuses were illustrated in chalk drawings by Struthers' wife. (My old 'Bishop', T. Struthers Symington, was named for J. P. Struthers. Symington's father had been a minister in Greenock.) I decided to revive this feature.

I raked through drawers of old blocks in the office, which had appeared in the *Telegraph* years before, and wrote captions for them. We worked up a pretty good page, and the teaching mission was really effective. The BBC became interested.

G

Ronnie Falconer, as he was then – now Dr Ronald F. Falconer, though distinction has made no difference to him – was head of religious programmes in Scotland; radio only, of course, at that time. He invited some of us up to do a radio discussion on the mission, its organization, and its effects. I was one of the speakers, though the first time they took a sound level the needle nearly bent in the middle. Tom Allan was the interviewer. It was the first time I had met that magic man.

I was not offered any engagements, but at least I now knew the man in charge, and we seemed to take to one another.

The year 1954 was the centenary of the founding of Cartsburn and I wrote to Ronnie and asked if we could have a broadcast service from the church to mark the occasion. He replied that we could have a broadcast, but not as a centenary commemoration. There was always some church having a centenary. A date was arranged.

Stanley Pritchard was to be in charge, and I asked him if it would be all right if I broadcast in Braid Scots. He was a bit doubtful, but he took a chance. I broadcast not only in Braid Scots but in Braid Scots verse. I won't call it poetry; it was just verse. It had a tremendous reception. I was asked back many times, and Cartsburn became so used to broadcasts that they became somewhat blasé about them. Which is something you must never do in broadcasting or, for that matter, in anything else.

People say to me: 'I'm sure you never get nervous.' Nervous! Anybody who goes before the public without feeling nervous isn't going to make much of a job of what he's doing.

There followed *Lift up your hearts* and in those days you had to be in the studio at half past seven in the morning each day. It wasn't recorded. And then the national network and *The People's Service*. The Post Office saw that this was happening so often from Cartsburn that they left up the wire which connected the church to the main line.

There were special services too: Christmas, New Year's eve, New Year's day. There were talks from the studio, and they all appeared to go down very well with listeners. I would like to think it was because of the content, but I know perfectly well that the voice had a lot to do with it.

Journalism had a lot to do with what success I've had in broad-casting, and playwriting too, of course. For one thing the feature writer has to learn to put up with is the sub-editor, who goes over his piece of immortal prose, and with his blue pencil deletes this and that and the other before the thing sees print.

I would read over a script to Ronnie or Stanley or Wilson Anderson, and they would say: 'You're two minutes over, Jimmy.' So I would do my own subbing, scoring out this sentence and that sentence, and this would amaze them. For others to whom they had said the same thing would, almost with tears in their eyes, protest that any deletion would completely ruin the whole thing. These were they who had never worked for newspapers.

Came television. It was quite a while after TV came to Scotland that we got a set. When the Test matches were on I got the key of a house in the parish and watched them there, doing a little visitation at the intervals. But eventually we acquired a set. One Sunday night there was a minister on, who was making (in my opinion, and I think my opinion is the opinion of the average layman) a dog's breakfast of the thing. I got so worked up about it that I wrote a letter to Ronnie in which I said that if I couldn't make a better job of it than that I would give up altogether.

I took the letter down to the pillar box on the corner and posted it. Then came back and wondered if I had killed my chances altogether. Even the heads of departments on the BBC don't like criticism, though they may appreciate it.

Ronnie offered me a chance on television, and warned me that I was taking altogether a bigger chance than apparently I thought. But here, again, the stage training with the Players paid off.

There has to be a boss, and the boss is the producer. The actor may have his idea of how the part should be played. If so, he goes to the producer and says: 'I would like to play it this way.' And the producer, if he has any sense, says in rehearsal: 'That's not the way I see it. I liked the way you played this bit and that bit, but overall, I want it played this way.' Then the actor, if he is sensible, says: 'OK if that's the way you want it, that's the way you'll get it.' And he plays his part without any grudge.

On my first performance on television, and believe me this is a nerve-racking business, Ronnie was producer, and he paid me a great compliment. He told me that mine had been a thoroughly professional performance. And this is the secret of it.

Maybe some folk think that you shouldn't approach the propagation of religion professionally, but they're wrong, completely wrong. It has to be done professionally (not 'professionally' in the sense that you're earning your living off it) otherwise it is an embarrassment to the viewer. There must be competence. The broadcaster comes to the producer with what he has to say. The producer thereupon tells him how he wants it said.

After the first there came the second and the third and the fourth and many others. We did a series for children on lighthouses, and buoys and the gun that won the West, with exhibits provided by the Kelvingrove Museum. We did a harvest thanksgiving from the studio, with the church choir providing the praise, and with the products of Greenock, rather than the produce of the farm as the focal point. Then came a New Year's day service from the church. It was a tremendous success, and all by sheer accident.

Andy Stewart and the White Heather Club were on just before us, and they rather overran their time. Andy must have been striving for that ultimate high note. So many singers sing a song too low so that they can finish on the high note.

There was no time for the credits, and the moment Andy's high note had died away, on came Dow's sepulchral tones. The viewer, even if capable at that time of night, had not had time to switch off. The congregation burst into 'A Guid New Year to ane and a'', and people wondered if this was a church at all, having this as the opening praise.

It changed into a hymn which I had written to the same tune: 'For Christ is King, the Lord of time and tide, the Life, the Truth, the Way.' Viewing figures for that service were very high, mainly for the reason mentioned in the previous paragraph. But Ronnie was impressed by the singing.'

There followed *Songs of Praise*. Ronnie asked me what my views were on songs of praise, and I told him that my selection of hymns would be hymns which folk knew and which they could sing away to themselves while they were listening, or at least hum if they had forgotten the words, and that there should be a fair sprinkling of Redemption hymns, whose theology isn't all that good, but which are so singable, and which tend to take people back to the age of innocence. He approved, and our *Songs of Praise* services were very well received.

We had one that was all male, with the excellent Greenock Male Voice choir as the centre piece and with the church packed with Cubs, Scouts, Lifeboys and Brigade. That was a service to remember, especially when we belted into 'Will your anchor hold'.

Ronnie was a genius at the use of cameras in a service like this, and usually had five of them operating. The man in the pulpit has to try to remember which one is on him when he is speaking, and it's not all that easy even if there is a wee red light on the front of the camera that is operating. When the BBC outside broadcasting unit appear on the scene, it's like the shows arriving at the fair, and, for reasons of economy, the BBC like to do two services when all the apparatus is present. They will do a morning service broadcast live, and then in the afternoon record a *Songs of Praise* for broadcast later on.

One Sunday we were doing this and I lost my voice. I had been over-rehearsing. I managed to get through the morning service by going very close to the microphone, and managed the introduction to the hymns in the afternoon.

On the Monday or Tuesday after the live broadcast of the morning service, I had a letter from a dear old lady who was very worried about my voice. She included an infallible recipe for getting rid of the state of my throat, though by the time the services were over I had the notion that it could be mended only by the application of a razor.

The *Songs of Praise* recording was broadcast about a couple of months later, and I got a most indignant letter from the same dear old lady. What had I done with her infallible cure? Here was I two months later, still croaking away like a bronchial crow, and not one little bit better! I should be ashamed of myself! I wrote her, and explained.

Scottish Television, the commercial channel, then appeared on the scene, and, naturally enough, as far as religious broadcasting was concerned, were inclined to invite men who had demonstrated with the BBC that they could do the job.

To begin with they had no religious broadcasting department;
they have had one for some years now, under Nelson Gray. Then
there was only an advisory committee, consisting mainly of ministers
under the chairmanship of Arthur Gray, who had been a year
behind me in college and a member of the celebrated Glasgow ministers' football team. They asked me to do a series of *Late Calls*.
This was to be recorded, since it is an expensive business to have a
whole team standing by at that time of night. I had already done
Epilogues for the BBC, which tend to come on too late at night.

I was a wee bit uneasy when I got this invitation, for here was
the rival channel and I was already well established with the BBC,
who would be entitled to say: 'We trained you and gave you your
start. Now you're cashing in.'

This thought occurred, but in fairness to myself I must say that
this was not the main consideration that I might fall out with the
BBC. I just don't like this TV image. I hate being called a television
personality, just as I hate being called an authority on Burns. I told
Ronnie Falconer of my misgivings.

He said: 'Look, Jimmy, this is something that is far bigger than
you or me. This is the Word, reaching a mass of people who will not
be reached in any other way. You have a talent for it. You've been
given it to use. Use it!'

I accepted the STV offer and in due course turned up at the
studio. The chaps in charge knew what they were about; they
knew more about broadcasting than I did, but they didn't know
as much about religious broadcasting and I had a feeling that
they didn't care all that much about it either. I read a script for
voice level and timing, and they were satisfied, though I think they
paid more attention to the voice level and the timing than they
did to the content. They explained the signs they would give if I
had to slow down or speed up. I would get signs for the minute,
half-minute, quarter-minute and closing five seconds. This is quite
normal. You've got to get used to people crawling about the floor
out of the camera's eye, and making gestures. We went ahead and
did all six in front of a fixed camera in a small room.

When they were done I went into the production room in time
to hear the producer say: 'Thank God for a professional.' Once
again I regarded that as a compliment.

A minister, be he broadcasting or not, is a professional: like a professional lawyer or a professional golfer. We can call ourselves professionals because we have worked at our craft and can do it better than the amateur can. The only difference is that we get paid less.

Other broadcasting there was too, which was not classed as religious. There was *Morning Call,* broadcast on radio at breakfast time, when I gave about three minutes of nonsense which people complained made them miss their bus. On the same programme was Effie Morrison, the district nurse in *Dr Finlay's Casebook.* It was a very popular programme which folk still talk about, but it just stopped, for no apparent reason.

These then, were the doors that Greenock opened to me, but it was not entirely a success story. There were setbacks and disappointments. I can't say, as Winston Churchill said, that I have no unfulfilled ambitions. After all, it isn't every man who can say that he had his first novel published on the day he qualified for the old-age pension.

30. Practical Stuff

While all this was going on, of course, the family was growing and growing up. There had never been any doubt about daughter Margaret's ambition, which was to be a nurse. It was not until much later, and after she had been sister in the Princess Elizabeth Hospital in Guernsey, had qualified as district nurse, then taken her diploma in social studies at Southampton University, and in the meantime got married, that she decided that she could easily have been a doctor if she had taken the notion while she was in school. I pointed out to her that had she done so she would not have met and married Douglas. She knew this already, but it's as well to be reminded of these things.

I had hoped to have a grandson who would play for Scotland but he isn't going to come from that side of the family. At the moment of writing we are waiting to discover what Eilidh is going to bring forth north of the border.

Tommy was born in 1944 with red hair. He now calls it auburn, but he must be a throwback. Living in the west end of Greenock, he naturally found his pals among the boys whose fathers earned a lot more than I did, but I can't remember him ever complaining. At an early age he displayed a real talent for acting, but never got very much credit for it. People just said: 'Well, after all, he's Jimmy Dow's son, isn't he?' Wisely he did not try to develop this talent.

This was the time of the notorious (at least I thought it was notorious) eleven-plus examination, when parents were making nervous wrecks of their progeny, not so much because they wanted them to get on in the world, but because it was 'the thing' to have them qualify for the top stream. It was something I did not set much store by, which may have been a reason why Tommy didn't either. On leaving school he signed on as an apprentice compositor with the *Greenock Telegraph*, did very well at the Glasgow School of Printing, and is now the firm's sales manager, earning a sight more than his father ever did. We took to Eilidh as soon as we met her. She has now given up teaching to have their first baby. The name Eilidh is pronounced Ailey and is the Gaelic for Helen. The trouble with the Gaels is that they can't spell. But with the arrival of the 1960s I was beginning to wonder if the time had not come for me to be moving on to a less demanding parish where I might end my days in a modicum of peace and quiet.

Cartsburn parish was a big one: 12,000 people at least, half or more of them being Roman Catholic. There was the old part of the parish, tall substantial tenements but showing their years. Apart from one block in Belville Street up above the church, there were no bathrooms, though most of the houses had inside toilets. There were no sinks on the landings or anything like that, but few had hot water.

Beyond Belville Street were other good tenements built under the far-sighted Artizans' Dwellings Act of nearly a hundred years before, and then, on the hill, and bisected by the Old Kilmacolm Road were the housing schemes built between the Wars, and not built very well.

A good many very decent folk lived in these schemes, and I was sorry for them, for many of their neighbours were of another sort, and gave them little chance to live the way they wanted to live. John Keats was very wise when he wrote: 'We are never so prone to quarrel with others as when we are dissatisfied with ourselves.' There are those who can't bear the sight of other folk doing what they know perfectly well they could do themselves if they took the time and the trouble. Vandalism was rife, and there was hardly an issue of the *Telegraph* which failed to tell the tale of what the magistrates or sheriff had to say about the inhabitants of 'The Strone'.

These new houses had been built mainly to accommodate those unhoused through slum clearance, and it was a bold attempt to deal with a situation which should have been dealt with years before. The central area of Greenock had been no credit to the civic fathers of the day.

The men and women of the earlier Labour town councils were idealists and must be given full credit for tackling a housing prob-

lem that had grown too big. But there is a practical side of idealism
and it is not enough to lift thousands of people out of a slum and
rehouse them together in modern homes. I've already said in an
earlier chapter that slums aren't houses. Slums are people.

It's always fatal to generalize, of course. Some of the rehoused
people snatched eagerly at the chance of a new way of living, but
often they were not given the chance. The life of a good family
living in a close with five other families who had no intention of
improving themselves and who resented the fact that there were
others who did not think along these lines, could be sheer misery.
Many complained bitterly that they had been shifted away from the
pub and the pawn and the pictures (bingo wasn't on the cards then).
This was not their kind of life. Therefore they would make sure
that nobody else enjoyed it either.

This kind of thing was not confined to Greenock, of course.
It was typical of all industrial towns. There's one housing scheme
in Paisley where they cannot persuade any new tenant to go at all.

The parish, then, was divided into two very distinct parts, and
as far as my work was concerned, into rather more than that.

There were the Cartsburn Augustine families: a fair number
lived outside the parish, but most lived in it. Grand folk they were,
though apart from a couple of school teachers, two or three in-
surance agents, and a few shopkeepers and office workers, the
men were, in the main, employed in the shipyards and engine
shops.

If they had one fault, it was a tendency to keep thinking of
Cartsburn as it had been in Depression days: a kind of poor rela-
tion of all the other churches in the town, except the east end
churches. When Cartsburn was made a parish in 1856 it was the
first in the east end, where more than half the population of the town
lived. The west end was stacked with churches, for when the Dis-
ruption took place in 1843, those who left the Auld Kirk built a
new Free Kirk for every parish kirk. In addition there were the
Relief churches whose origins lay in another dispute. There were
Congregationalists and Baptists and Episcopalians, and they all
built in the west end, for that's where the people lived who were
in the habit of going to church. The east end was completely neglected except for missions run by the west end churches.

My officebearers tended to think that they were doing well if they could manage to keep the kirk's head above water and pay their way, but they could hardly be expected to meet the commitments to the Church of Scotland, as these were required of them. I didn't think this was good enough. They were just as able as most of the other congregations to play their full part. Although there were some pretty well-off congregations in Greenock, where, according to my predecessor James Francis, the retired Christians worshipped. Gradually the officebearers came round to this idea. We began to get a better conceit of ourselves. Attendances got better and better.

Of course we had gimmicks. You've got to have gimmicks, without, of course, losing sight of what the whole thing is about. We started a full attendance Sunday once a month with everybody there from babies in prams to grannies. We had musical services with well-known professional singers like Janette Sclanders and Alex Carmichael. We used drama. I chose topical subjects for evening service and advertised them well.

One sheriff, leaving Greenock, referred to the town as 'This unsavoury burgh'. I advertised this as my subject and the church was full. Even John Keane was there and he reported the sermon at length.

By this time in the summer, I was playing bowls on the Victoria green, where many of my men were members. I suggested a bowlers' service to the local bowling association, and this was taken up enthusiastically.

In church we planned for the future. Nothing had been done in the way of repairs, painting, decorating and the like during the War years. The lavatory facilities were negligible. Church members of former years must have been men of mighty bladders. We got a building fund going, with an eye to our centenary.

There are those who say, and maybe rightly, that a church should be able to do all it has to do, and more, through the weekly givings of the people. There shouldn't be any need for sales of work and jumble sales and basket teas and beetle drives and concerts and shows and 'special efforts'. That's all very well, but that's not how things go.

And, apart from anything else, if you want a congregation to be a community and a unity you must have objects to work for. This gets people involved and that's what you want.

Just after the war we had one sale of work which raised over five hundred pounds. Of course we had raffles, and continued to have raffles till the General Assembly said 'No raffles', and I stopped them amid shouts of protest. The logically-minded members said what was the difference between raffles and guessing how many peas are in a jar, or the weight of the cake or the name of the doll. There is no difference, I told them. But we are a Presbyterian church and as a Presbyterian church we do what the General Assembly tells us to do. And that was that. Mind you, I think that there were still some wee private raffles organized on the side. I did not inquire.

The Roman Catholics are logical. They have raffles, and somebody must have said to the priest in St Laurence's: 'If you're going to have raffles you might as well run a football pool.' So they ran a football pool which was won several times by members of mine.

Then we discovered dry rot in the hall floor. The hall had been lying unused all through the War. The whole floor, with the joists, would have to be renewed.

Quite a number of the men were joiners in Scott's, Lithgow's and the Greenock Dockyard. They put their heads together and offered to re-lay the floor in hardwood if the church would buy the wood. I laboured with them and pretended I was dafter than I am. There's nothing gives a chap more pleasure than the discovery that he can do something the minister can't do. For the finishing touches we worked all night for a couple of nights, and got the session clerk's wife out of bed to give us our breakfast.

We cleared out the old pulpit which was a thing like the bridge of a ship, built a new choir range, and a new pulpit in memory of James Francis. One of the elders, John Taylor, who'd had pictures exhibited in the Scottish Academy, carved a panel of the face of James Francis which was built into the front of the pulpit. The pulpit maker offered him a job on the spot. He didn't take it. He was a plater.

Then we built our new halls at a cost of seven thousand pounds and wondered what to do next. This is practical stuff, of course, but isn't the whole work of the church practical? This is what builds a congregation and welds the people together and holds them together. The trouble was we were getting too inward-looking.

31. The Years of Living

There was still the more or less untouched part of the parish. We weren't doing enough about it. We were in need of some missionary enterprise, to bring those people into the fold.

Shortly after coming to Cartsburn I had heard rumour of a small Sunday School that was meeting in a disused hut across the railway. I found out more about it and went to have a look.

It seemed that in the summer of 1943 the Presbytery had decided to have an open air Sunday School in the Strone Farm scheme in the parish, and had put in charge of it one James Anderson.

James was one of the men, and there are plenty of them, who dearly would have loved to be a minister, but who had never had the chance. He had a job, but that was only to fill in the time. His real life was in church work and missions. He had been in charge of the Foundry Boys Bible class in Greenock, and the Foundry Boys was one of the great institutions in its day; though, like many another similar body, its day is over. He had decided to try to keep a parish Sunday School going during the winter. I found them shivering, and thereupon led them down the hill to the small hall of the church. I had no objection to an outside body working in the parish. but this was really the church's business.

That Sunday School grew faster than the congregation's Sunday School grew. The church, however, was a good half-mile from the Strone scheme and I negotiated for the use of an old half-derelict villa which had once been somebody's pride and joy, and which stood, or leaned against, the scheme. It masqueraded occasionally as a community centre. Thither we moved, James in charge (I was regarded as his assistant). I played the hymns and choruses on what was left of a piano, and we had a small band of devoted teachers. I'm afraid Cartsburn, with a few honourable exceptions, did not evince a great deal of interest in the venture, and were shocked when I told them they would have to give financial support. They were not markedly missionary minded. But I told them that if they would not do the work of the parish they would have to finance it. They did. They had no alternative.

The work prospered, and through it I got my foot into many doors. Of course the people of the parish came for the usual offices when these were required.

Over the year I would average about ten parish funerals a month, and this takes time. You have to see the folk before the funeral; there is the funeral itself, very often on a Saturday when Morton were playing at home (but first things first) and there had to be a visit afterwards, and more visits if I thought that there was a family something might be made of. More often it wasn't. I had no car.

There were babies to be baptized, which raised the problem: 'When does a minister baptize and when doesn't he?' I consulted R. J. Mackay, a splendid man who was Presbytery clerk. He was minister of the old Free Gaelic, now St Columba's. He thought in Gaelic and translated it into English.

I asked him about baptism. His advice, as always, was very wise.

'Every child is entitled to baptism,' he told me. 'But not every parent is fit to take the vows of baptism. If you are not satisfied about the parents, you must find someone who will stand in loco parentis. But remember that a baptizing church is a catechizing church, and that the responsibilities of the congregation do not end when the sacrament has been administered.'

This is something which has not been sufficiently impressed upon kirk sessions, or which kirk sessions do not want to be impressed with: that once a child has been baptized a large part of the responsibility for the spiritual well-being of that child falls upon the kirk session. And this is what the Strone Farm Sunday School was largely all about.

Very often the baby was illegitimate, which isn't the baby's fault. More often there had been a 'mixed marriage' which resulted in a husband and wife who had never gone to church remaining consistent and continuing not to go to church. And yet some of the best members I had in Cartsburn had started off their wedded life in a mixed marriage.

At this time the Assembly were producing White Papers on baptism, apparently written by men who had never seen a parish like mine. I moved in Presbytery once that we should recommend that the next White Paper should be written in English. But where there is a big Roman Catholic population there is bound to be an attitude to baptism which we would consider sheer superstition. Nevertheless, allowances must be made.

I've sat for an hour in a house where the infant's mother was still confined to bed but was anxious to have the baby baptized, trying to explain what it was all about, and when she had agreed, have baptized the child, only to hear her say: 'Thank God, Mr Dow, I aye think they dae better efter they're done.'

Now and again there would be a phone call: would I go to the Rankin Memorial Hospital and baptize a baby who was seriously ill. You don't refuse this kind of request. You know it won't make any difference to the baby but it can make a whole lot of difference to the mother.

But if that baby got well, my old friend Jimmy Baxter who was in charge of the maternity hospital and who had supervised the birth of some 25 000 babies, would get no credit for it. It was: 'The minute Mr Dow christened the wee pet you could see her gettin' better.'

There were so many baptisms that we had to set aside the first Sunday of the month, after sermon, for the sacrament. Parents were supposed to let me know, but being aware of the statutory time, some would slip in at the end of the queue, with the baby carried by a neighbour, or even by a twelve-year-old sister all on her own. This just about drove the beadle off his nut, for he had to receive them and keep them in the vestry till the appropriate time.

There were marriages too; plenty of marriages even with Scottish registrars now entitled to conduct the ceremony. There still remained that wee something: to be married by a minister gives the marriage a better chance.

Manse weddings were pretty well out by this time, much to the relief of ministers' wives. It was either the church or the vestry, though in our new halls we had incorporated a small chapel for the purpose, used at other times as the session house. The reception thereafter would be in some local hotel, or tea room, or in the Masonic

Hall, the Shepherds' Hall or the like with an 'outside caterer'. They always served steak pie.

They were happy years and they were sad years, though they could not be classified as such in years on the calendar, for the years of living do not follow the dates on the calendar. Happy years when I saw the youngsters growing up and getting married and raising their own families with the church still at the centre of things. And sad years when I saw my old folk getting older, and me along with them.

There are times when all that a minister can say to folk is: 'There's nothing I can say to you.' For he knows how true the platitude is (and words don't become platitudes unless they are true) that 'Time is the great healer'. Of course time is the great healer, but any minister who says that at the time of bereavement shouldn't be in his job.

After a while he can say: 'Look, life will never be the same again and you wouldn't want to think that it could. But that does not mean to say that it can never be happy again. A different kind of happiness, but still, happiness.' In time they find that this is true. If it were not true, life would be unbearable. This, to me, is what the priesthood of all believers is, though this is not what it means theologically.

Misfortune comes, trouble, illness, death and sorrow, and of course the first reaction is 'Why me? Why should I be singled out for this? Why should this happen to me? I've lived the good life, I've done my best all my days. And this comes to me! Why not to so-and-so? – who has taken the line of least resistance all his life, never done a thing for other folk, and never gone to church, and there he is flourishing like the green bay tree. Why me?'

This person feels lonely and isolated. There's some idea of a judgement, but they can't understand why there should be any judgement. (As a matter of fact there isn't any, but you don't bring that up.)

Then they get over things a wee bit, and they make their way (and this takes a conscious effort) back to church, and what do they see? They see one here and one there who has passed through the same valley of the shadow, and who has kept going, trusting in the rod and staff, and who has come out at the other side into the light again. They see those who faced the same problem and who found the answer because they endured; who trusted that if you throw yourself into the everlasting arms, they will never let you down.

So the loneliness goes, and they see that, for those who have never known that loneliness, they themselves are the witnesses: the people who have walked in darkness. They themselves are the proof of the faith that they got from the others. Instead of being takers, now they are givers. This is, to me at least, though I have no doubt that theologically this is all wrong, the meaning of the priest-hood of all believers.

This is what a congregation is. If it isn't that, it just isn't a congregation. It's no more than a group of people in something not much different from any secular organization devoted to good works. I can lay hand on heart and affirm that in forty years I have learned more from my people than ever they have learned from me. And I have told them so.

I have been with them in their troubles, supposed to be bringing them comfort, and the question that has been big in my mind has been: 'It's all very well for you, mate, saying this and that. But what would you be like if you were facing what they are facing? I hope and pray that I would have made as good a witness as they did.

In Glasgow, in my old assistantship days, I don't know how often I sat in a horse-drawn carriage with a father in the opposite seat, holding on his knees a wee white coffin with his baby in it. I simply could not even begin to know what that chap was feeling until our own first child was born.

This book was supposed to be reasonably light-hearted, but there is too much in a minister's life that is not light-hearted. I hope and trust that I have never neglected to give my people the benefit of my experience. But I shudder to think how little that experience was in the early days.

In the ministry, a man must always be learning. He must be continually asking himself if the sanction for doing something in a particular way is that he has been taught that this is the right way to do it. I did not learn one single thing in college about dealing with death in a home that has been of the very slightest use to me

since. And if it wasn't of the slightest use to me, it is a certainty
that it wasn't of the slightest use to the people I was there to minister
to.

For example: the conventional thing to do in a home where
there has been a death is to have prayer. There's a time and place
for everything.

If the minister is there when death occurs (as I very often was)
or immediately afterwards, prayer will help to compose the bereaved
(as long as the words 'Thy will be done' are not used).

If he gets there when the friends and neighbours have gathered,
as Scots people do in their kindly way, and the woman next door
has made the cup of tea, and they've sent out for the Madeira cake,
he sits and chats with the widow, who has been going over all the
circumstances of the death with all the neighbours, but who has
now got control of herself with a very conscious effort. The boys
of the family have set their chins firmly. They are not going to let
their mother down.

Then the minister says: 'Shall we have a word of prayer?' Not
because he thinks this will do any good, but because he feels this
is expected of him. And before he's half-way through, the widow
has broken down and the boys are crying, and ashamed because
they are crying. There's a time and place for everything, but it's
got to be the right time and the right place. And the sensible – or
maybe the sensitive – minister, is the one who ought to know when
and where that time and place are.

Usually the minister does far better to talk straightforwardly
about the man and the reminiscences that he has of the man (or the
wife or mother or father, for that matter) and then to take the
relict (what a horrible word) into the lobby, for often there are
only the two rooms and the coffin is lying in the other, and to say:
'I'll be over tomorrow morning at eleven; will you look out your
papers,' and you tell them what papers they'll need, 'and we'll go
down to the registrar's,' and the registrar was a member of the same
bowling green as I was, 'and then we'll go down to the Ministry of
Pensions and get all your business straightened out.'

This is the kind of guidance that folk need in these extremities
and this isn't done by prayer. People have got to keep their feet
on the ground. You do that, and then you take her to a tea room

for a cup of tea and a scone and have a blether about practical things. She begins to realize that one kind of life has come to an end and that another way of life has started.

But I've heard at second-hand, or even at third-hand: 'You know, Mr Dow came in to see her when we were there, and he never offered up a word of prayer.' I'll have prayer with the bereaved. But not with an audience.

32. The Call to Arran

There's been a bit of encircling gloom in these last chapters, and the reader may think that he or she is being made to suffer from my efforts to give some advice to young ministers, none of whom will be able to afford to buy this book anyway, though without being immodest, I would suggest it would do them more good than many of their prescribed and recommended volumes.

But as we come near the close of these rambling reminiscences we'd better try to lighten the gloom a little. There are odd things that spring to the mind.

Like the undertaker on the south side of Glasgow away back in the Union Church days, when the funeral was often in a single-end, with the coffin lying, always open, on the dresser. I would conduct the service, and give him a sign that I was finished. Whereupon the family, followed by the friends and relations, would gather round to pay 'their last respects'.

The undertaker would then produce from a pocket which must have been modelled on the pocket in which a joiner keeps his three-foot rule, an enormous screwdriver, accompanied by the words, 'Well, are youse all quite sa'isfied?'

Like my favourite character, Horatio Hornblower, I have always found it hard to suppress a giggle. I always wanted to ask him what we were supposed to be satisfied about? Was it my ministrations? Was it his professional services? Or were we well assured that the chap in the coffin was dead?

There was the class in English that I ran for my church youngsters who were going up for 'O' grade or Highers, and who were scared that they might not be 'presented'. What this 'presentation' business is all about I don't know. When youngsters have put in the requisite time at school they are surely entitled to have a bash at the examinations. After all the less bright have as good a chance of hitting on a paper that suits them as the more talented have of hitting on a paper which doesn't.

I had one lad in my class one year who was very doubtful about his English. He thought he would fail in the preliminary examination in school. He passed, he got his highers, went to university, sailed through his medical classes and is now a prominent surgeon in Glasgow. Others are teachers, lawyers, chartered accountants. I don't say they wouldn't have passed if I hadn't coached them, but the simple fact is that they did pass.

They made me moderator of Greenock Presbytery in Coronation year. You get this distinction for long service and good conduct. It meant, however, that we got an invitation to the royal garden party at Holyroodhouse. The first time we were at the garden party was when I was in Barony North. The Queen's mother and father were there that year. I thought I recognized some of the sandwiches. On that first occasion I wore the tile hat and frock coat. On the last occasion an ordinary coat and hat. The tile hat had been used in *Bunty Pulls the Strings* and had not been seen since.

When we came to Greenock in 1943 Margaret's Aunt Maggie was retiring as a housekeeper in Doune. She was seventy, and having been a housekeeper for many years (she was a widow) had no home. We had plenty of room and she came to stay with us. It was a good arrangement for we had to be out a lot at nights, and Tommy was a baby. He was her golden-haired boy. I used to have a horse of the same colour. Aunt Maggie was with us till she died over ninety years old.

Mother was living in Rochdale with Elsie, whose husband George (one of my Barony North lads) was secretary of John Bright's mills. They lived in John Bright's house, which was a building of historic importance. George, alas, died some years ago. But Mother would come up for a holiday once or twice a year, and the two kept one another company. But this was not the end of the Forsyth Street guest house, or old peoples' home.

Margaret's father had retired from J. and P. Coats in 1941. He was a famous fisher and breeder of cocker spaniels, and many a weary hour I spent rowing him over the Carron Loch in Stirlingshire. He and Margaret's stepmother took a house in Bridge of Weir, but in the mid-fifties they both took ill.

We brought them down to Greenock by ambulance, for Margaret couldn't travel up there every day, and after a while we went into conference, for it was plain what when they recovered they wouldn't be able to look after themselves. We converted the big sitting room into a bed-sitting room, and they moved in. He loved it.

Every Friday he took a trip up to Paisley, where Margaret's brother Bert had a prosperous butcher's business, and would come back with his wee case full of meat and a half-bottle of whisky which he hid so carefully from his wife that he had trouble finding it again. He had a dram every night and was, I am sure, persuaded that it was still his half-bottle he was drinking on the Saturday.

When Mother came on holiday, the combined ages of the four of them was something like three hundred and twenty. Of course, ours was a big house, with attic bedrooms where Tommy slept, and daughter Margaret and her pals from Glasgow Royal when they were off duty. We had room to do what a great many other people could not do, though they had the will to do it. When our doctor, John Campbell, called, which was frequently, he would walk in and ask which ward it was this time. It was a lot of work for Margaret but we would not have had it any other way.

Their presence was not the only reason why I stayed so long in Greenock, though it was one of the reasons. Greenock still holds a large part of my heart.

Occasionally a vacancy committee would arrive from somewhere or another, and come round to the vestry to ask all sorts of questions to ascertain if I was the man for them. I would then ask them some questions about attendance at their pre-communion service (our attendance was around three hundred) and how many elders were Sunday School teachers. It became very embarrassing for them, but I enjoyed it hugely, since I had no intention of leaving Cartsburn anyway.

They were expecting questions about stipend, and if there was central heating in the manse. The only question I ever asked about stipend was whether they were offering more than they paid their last man.

This is a most hurtful thing that congregations do, though I'm sure they do it unthinkingly, and ministers are not supposed to have feelings like other people. But it is hurtful to work in a place for twenty years, then leave and find that the congregation are offering a couple of hundred a year more to somebody they don't know than they paid to one they had known all these years. This happened to me when I left Greenock.

What we need in the Church of Scotland is 'direction'. This amateurish business of choosing a minister on the strength of a couple of sermons is sheer nonsense. And another reason for having some kind of direction is that now and again a minister needs a change, but he doesn't want it to be a permanent change.

After twenty years in an industrial charge, he could do with five years somewhere smaller and quieter. But what he's afraid of is that if he goes, say, to one of the Western Isles, he'll be left there for the rest of his life. The Church ought to be able to say to him: 'Look, old chap, you've been bashing your brains out here for a long time, how would you like to go to Islay for a year or two? After that we'll fix you up in town again to get on with the work you do best.'

What difference this would make not only to the man but to the rural church which probably has been standing vacant for years or which has been ministered to by a series of young probationers who are just learning their job.

One solid offer came which sorely tempted me. That was Southend, Kintyre, where my old friend 'The Padre', Angus MacVicar's father, had ministered for fifty years. I took my Boys' Brigade down there a lot, and always preached for him.

'You are the man to follow me here, James,' he would say. 'When I retire the charge is yours if you want it.' The thing was as simple and straightforward as that.

One morning the letter came, and I knew that all I had to do was lift the phone and say 'Yes.' All the Southend folk knew me through the church and the camp and the drama. But it was not to be. Margaret was still training in Glasgow and Tommy was still in school, and we had the old folk. But that was not the main reason and I wouldn't like Tommy to think that I had made the supreme sacrifice on his behalf, for there was not much that he could do on Kintyre when he left school.

I just felt that I was too young to leave a place where I was doing good work and where I felt I was needed, not just in Cartsburn, but in the Presbytery and the town. There was still too much to give. I wrote the Padre and I phoned Angus who nearly burst out greeting. I think he had in mind a union of Dow and MacVicar beside which Morecambe and Wise, Marks and Spencer, and even Ham and Haddie would have remained forever in obscurity.

Then one by one in the early sixties the old folk died, and I knew that the house where they had lived so long was no longer the same place for Margaret. Old Tom went first, then Aunt Maggie, then my mother who was living with us at the time, and finally Margaret's stepmother.

The call to Lochranza and Pirnmill came entirely out of the blue. Bob Carmichael, minister at Brodick, knew that usually I had a couple of Sundays free in July. We united in July and August with the neighbouring East Congregational church, which gave all the hired servants a month off. I had taken services for Bob when I had the BB on Arran. He phoned to ask if I could take a Sunday at Lochranza and Pirnmill. Two separate churches, but the same sermon does both. I said I would, blissfully unaware of the fact that the charge was vacant.

In the afternoon the officebearers (and there weren't very many of them) put their heads together and popped the question. Would I come as their minister? I said I had no ambitions in that direction and went home to Greenock, where I mentioned, quite casually, that the Arran charge was vacant and that it seemed to be mine if I wanted it.

Margaret told me to apply for it. I asked what was to happen with Tommy, who still had a year of his time to do as a compositor. That was arranged by Margaret in two minutes. Robert and Molly Goodwin would take Tommy. Things were running away with me. I wrote the letter of application. Later, Margaret asked me if I had posted it. I said I had not. She held out her hand for the thing, took it, went down to the pillar box and posted it. And that was that. I preached as sole nominee. The congregation was not large, for my predecessor, poor soul, had been ill for years and had had to retire on health grounds.

There was a Greenock church once which was vacant, and they were going round hearing applicants. They heard this chap and went round to the vestry afterwards for the usual interview. The minister suggested that since a most important decision was pending, they should open the meeting with prayer. The vacancy committee was greatly impressed by this evidence of faith and piety. They reported back accordingly and it was decided that this chap should be invited to Greenock to be heard by the whole congregation.

They were prepared to call him, but he turned it down because his wife didn't like the manse. A question of faith and works, with faith losing as usual. We accepted the call without ever having seen the manse. It might have been an enormous old house that needed a squad of servants, but it turned out to be a very pleasant place, not too big, but adequate to accommodate the family in the summer time, and all the other folk who had decided that Arran was a nice place for a holiday.

That was in the autumn of 1965, and a boat-load of Cartsburners came down for the induction, and here was I, after more than thirty years of the town, chasing red deer off my turnips.

The old Cartsburn parish is still there, of course, with the church on the brow of the brae, which was so kenspeckle, now dwarfed by the multi-storey flats which have replaced the old tenements. This was really why I left. It was no longer my place.

My successor asked me several times to come back to take a service but I always refused. He left after five years and the assistant – they now had a full-time layman assistant – asked me to take a communion service, and I agreed. It was all very nostalgic with a 'will ye no' come back again' atmosphere. If I had hinted that I would come back I'm quite sure they would have offered me the job, and, financially it was a better job than it had been when I left, but I was quite blunt about it. I told them I was part of Cartsburn's past, not of its future, and the only way to be part of the future of anything is to be part of its past.

Of Lochranza and Pirnmill I'm not going to write anything, for I still have to live here. I thought that by coming here I would be getting away from some problems, but have discovered that not only do they have the same problems in Arran, but that they have invented one or two I had never heard of.

I was still doing a fair amount of broadcasting, and brought this with me. We had *The People's Service* several times from the church.

Indeed we had broadcasts so often that the Post Office telephone people decided to leave a permanent connection to the vestry. But the great day was when the television outside broadcasting unit arrived for a *Songs of Praise* on the castle green. It was like the shows, and was the biggest thing to happen in Lochranza since Bruce saw the spider. There isn't so much broadcasting since Ronnie Falconer left the BBC. He liked my way of doing things, and his successors are well entitled to entrust this most important part of their work to younger men.

When I go back to Greenock (I'm writing a modern history of the town at the behest of the corporation) people ask me how I'm enjoying my retirement, and how do I manage to fill in the time, and how do I get on with the natives? Little do they know. For one thing there are fewer 'natives' than there are incomers in the villages. Archie, a retired doctor, calls us the white settlers. With the age of retirement getting lower all the time, more and more are leaving the mainland rat-race and seeking the peace of the quiet places and an amazing number of them are from south of the border.

There was a time when every house that fell vacant was snapped up (often at a ridiculous price) by people who simply wanted a summer house. This is changing. They are coming here to stay, and they are people of some consequence. I don't mean that they are people with plenty of money, but they are people who have held down responsible jobs on the mainland and in foreign parts, and conversations are by no means parochial or parish pump, but informed and 'meaty'. And almost all of them are very much inclined to the church, which keeps me well on my toes.

Then there are the local interests. I'm secretary of the Improvements Association, secretary of the village hall committee, was district councillor, and then county councillor, vice-chairman of the Buteshire education committee, and chairman of the Arran education sub-committee. I've now been adopted as prospective Liberal candidate for Arran, Cumbrae, Largs and West Kilbride on the new Strathclyde Region which will be set up in the new order of local govenment. By the time this book is published I'll know whether I've been elected or not.* Time, in other words, does not

*I wasn't!

hang heavily on my hands. I still write leaders for the *Greenock Telegraph*, and since these have to be phoned in before the morning papers arrive I'm usually awake at seven to hear the news. I hasten to add I don't get up then. I go early to bed.

Being now sixty-six, I could retire, but I don't see the point. For one thing I'd have to get a house somewhere, and it would take me all my time to afford a hen-house. But the main reason is that I can still do my day's work and preach a reasonable sermon, and as long as I have my health and strength and the folk want me to stay, I'll stay.

And there are no signs as yet that my people are not content with me, though as one of the younger men said when I asked him why he did not come to church: 'To tell the truth, sir James, I don't come because I'm frightened I might get to like it.'

Perhaps now that this discourse is off my chest I'll start writing about life on Arran. I can assure you that if it is ever published it will be published posthumously.

Index